The Best of German Cooking

HENRIETTA HILTON

The Best of Scandinavian Cooking

KERSTIN SIMON LONDON

THE BEST OF GERMAN COOKING
first published 1964 *by*
ARLINGTON BOOKS LONDON
© *Henrietta Hilton* 1964

THE BEST OF SCANDINAVIAN COOKING
first published 1968 *by*
ARLINGTON BOOKS LONDON
© *Kerstin Simon London* 1968

THIS REPRINTED EDITED EDITION 1974

ISBN 0 7196 0318 8

ABBEY LIBRARY
CRESTA HOUSE HOLLOWAY ROAD
LONDON N7 8DE

The Best of German Cooking

HENRIETTA HILTON

Abbey Library

LONDON

The American Standard Cup measure is equivalent to the British Standard Cup, that is to say that they are both ½ pint cups, but the liquid measure for the American cup is 8 fluid oz, and the British cup 10 fluid oz.

	American liquid measure	British liquid measure
½ pint	8 fluid oz.	10 fluid oz.
1 pint	16 fluid oz.	20 fluid oz.
2 tablespoons	1 fluid oz.	2 fluid oz.

DRY INGREDIENT MEASURES

	American cup	British cup
Butter, margarine, fat or lard	8 oz.	8 oz.
Currants, sultanas, etc.	5 oz.	6 oz.
Bread-crumbs, fresh	1½ oz.	3 oz.
Bread-crumbs, dry	3½ oz.	6 oz.
Flour	4 oz.	5 oz.
Grated cheese	4 oz.	4 oz.
Honey, treacle, syrup	11 oz.	14 oz.
Icing sugar	4½ oz.	4½ oz.
Sugar, granulated or castor	7½ oz.	8 oz.
Rice	8 oz.	8 oz.
Cornflour	6 oz.	6 oz.

This introduction to German Cookery is aimed at the British woman (or man) who can already cook in English. I hope that the book will be bought by many of those who, having spent holidays in Germany, may be interested to reproduce some of the dishes they have enjoyed on their travels. It is not intended as a highly specialised treatise on German cooking as practised by the old-fashioned *hausfrau*. There is still a diminishing number of these who disdain any of the modern short cuts, preferring to make everything at home.

In dealing with the cooking of so large a country, a book of this scope cannot do more than describe the better-known dishes, and the author is humbly aware that a great deal of ground is left uncovered. Poultry and game, for example. In deciding what to leave out, it seemed to me that while the ubiquitous chicken on automatic spits holds sway, as it also does in Germany, a great many people will prefer to go on buying ready-cooked chickens. Moreover, a roasted bird is very much the same in any language.

Anyone who has recently visited Germany will know that self-service stores and pre-prepared eatables out of the deep-freezers, are as widely found there as they are here, and from these the clever cook can devise her own short-cuts for the recipes which follow. However, I hope many will find pleasure in following them the hard way.

The tourist in Germany will also have discovered how widely dishes vary in the different regions. We are familiar with the differences between the methods of the housewife in London, Manchester, Edinburgh and Belfast, and Germany, with her much larger territory, has a far greater variety. Moreover she has absorbed and adapted many of the dishes of the countries on her borders, and dishes from the far East in a way we islanders cannot imagine.

Despite this international tendency however, there are certain characteristics about genuine German native cooking which are so deeply ingrained that they will never change, and these are the types of food covered by the recipes which follow. Certain indigenous flavours, like the use of dill in salads and sauces, the ubiquitous pickled gherkin, the endless variety of sausages, and the universal devotion to pork and veal, are truly national.

Although vast areas of Germany are a long way from the sea, fish is eaten freely, fresh-water fish, lake fish, carp, are all prized for their nutritious value. In the top-class restaurants, fish is flown daily from the coast, and eaten, fresh from the sea, for lunch on the same day.

As in France, restaurant menus do not feature a great variety of puddings and pies. Sweets based on pancake batter and served in portions so large as to overwhelm the English visitor can always be ordered, but I have noticed that the German patrons order little from that end of the menu.

Fresh fruit, fruit compotes, and ices of enormous size and great elaboracy, are always available, and the numerous cafés serve a delectable assortment of rich cream cakes and *Torte* which cater very adequately for the sweet-tooth.

However, the housewife with hungry children to feed, still cooks the batters, boiled puddings and dumplings which her grandparents and great-grandparents gave to their children, and, for the benefit of her British counterpart, I have included some of each in this book.

Anyone familiar with French and Viennese and Swiss *patisserie* will have some idea of the richness and variety of German cakes and *Torte*. In the mountain districts, notably in the Black Forest, and the Bavarian Alps, where the grass grows so fast and so lush that they cut a hay crop at least three or four times during the summer, there is an abundance of rich cream, and this is lavishly used in confectionery. The synthetic creams and whips of the average, small British baker would not be tolerated over there. German *konditorei* rivals that of the Viennese, and portions served are even larger!

Finally, if you want to reproduce a genuine German dish in any of the categories which follow, do not economise on butter, eggs and cream, and do try to include any herbs specified. Otherwise you will be disappointed in the results, and the dishes will taste very much the same as many you already know. Every cook modifies every recipe we know, but flavouring, and high quality ingredients are always worth while. If you *must* cut down on eggs, use extra butter, and if you *must* cut down on butter (cheap butter costs very little more than margarine) use cheese curd for extra fat content. Several recipes, where curd has been used to save on butter, are included.

It is worth going to a little trouble to obtain the various ring-tins, spring-moulds, and shaped pudding boilers, described. Any good iron-monger, or large store should be prepared to get them for you, if not stocked. They are all obtainable in London, and, I daresay, in other large cities. The unfamiliar appearance of a dish can add enormously to its attraction.

Clear Soups and Broths

These are very popular in Germany and on all *table d'hôte* menus in restaurants and cafés, the first item is the *Tagessuppe*—the soup for the day. The various clear broths are served piping hot, well-seasoned and in comparatively small portions, and are intended, as appetisers. They are the ideal opening to a meal where the main dish is rich or heavy, for they stimulate the gastric juices, and, to some extent, they help to dilute what follows.

The various soup noodles, tiny dumplings, fried batter droplets and so on, which appear at the bottom of the soup plate, are dealt with at *Garnishes and Additions for Soups*. If you intend to use any of them, do not salt the soup until after they are in, as some of those bought ready-made are already salted.

The cook with access to a kitchen-garden, or allotment will always have supplies of what the German cook refers to as 'soup greens' and which some English cooks call 'pot herbs'. The standard German version consists of one leek, one small head of celery, one root of parsley, one parsnip (chopped or grated), and a chopped and browned onion, but any other root vegetables, and any fresh herbs you fancy, can be included. The brown outer skin of onions is left on and chopped up with the rest, for this helps to colour and to clear the liquid.

Chives or parsley, finely chopped, are dropped onto the surface of the liquid just before serving. To improve the quality of any soup or broth a piece of butter is placed on the soup plate and the hot liquid poured over it.

If wine is added it is not boiled with the soup, but added just before serving. If you decide to include a bunch of herbs for flavouring, these should go in for the last half hour of cooking, not longer.

If a dark brown liquid is required, fry the onion first until dark brown.

CLEAR MEAT BROTH

½ lb beef (any of the cheaper, leaner cuts. Skirt is good)
1 slice of ox liver, or heart
1 onion (with skin)
Soup greens (see above) as available
2–3 pints water
Beef bones
Salt

Well wash and scrub the root vegetables and cut them up, but not too finely. Wash the bones and cut up the meat and liver or heart. Put all the ingredients into cold salted water, cover the pan tightly and simmer gently for at least 1½ hours. Strain carefully. Some cooks add a little nutmeg. If desired, the beef can be cut into very small pieces and a good tablespoonful added to each portion of soup. If you are using soup noodles, boil them until tender in salted water, and add one tablespoonful to each portion.

CLEAR MEAT BROTH (A quicker variant)

½ lb finely minced fat beef
2 teaspoons any good meat extract
2–3 pints cold water
Soup greens and 1 large onion, put through the mincer

2 oz soup noodles (i.e. alphabet noodles)
Nutmeg if liked

Put all the ingredients into cold, salted water. Bring to the boil, and simmer for at least fifteen minutes (half an hour is better). Strain and cook the noodles for five minutes in the boiling soup.

BONE BROTH

2 lb beef bones (cooked bone leftovers can also be used)
4–5 pints water
Soup greens as available, but always include a leek, the green tops of celery, one or two onions and a large carrot

Get the butcher to chop the bones if very large, and wash them if necessary. Put them in the cold water (without salt) and simmer gently for at least three hours. Then add the cleaned, diced vegetables, and let the mixture go on simmering for another hour. Strain and salt to taste.

This liquor will be cloudy and is best used as the base for a thick soup. It is highly nourishing, but does not keep well in hot weather. If no refrigerator is available, it should be boiled for a few moments each morning, until used up.

VEGETABLE BROTH

This recipe uses lovage, a little known, but very old English herb, still found in some cottage gardens. It is exceedingly bitter, but if you can lay your hands on any, a small sprig gives a bite to the broth.

1 oz fat (butter, pork fat, or margarine)
Small sprig of lovage
1 large carrot
1 leek
2 roots of parsley
½ head of celery
2–3 pints cold water
Salt

Thoroughly wash and clean the vegetables, and chop them up, but not too finely. The onion should be quartered. Melt the fat in the bottom of the saucepan in which you intend making the soup and fry all the vegetables, keeping them well-stirred and shaken, to prevent sticking. Add the cold water and the lovage. Cover the pan tightly and simmer very slowly for two hours If you allow it to boil fast, the mixture will become cloudy. Strain and season to taste. Some of the vegetables, finely shredded, can be added to each portion when serving.

CHICKEN BROTH

1 *boiling fowl*
4½–6 *pints water*
Salt
1 *onion (with skin)*
Soup greens as available
Parsley
1 *leaf lovage*

Clean and chop the vegetables, leaving the brown skin on the onion, and put with the parsley and lovage into cold salted water, and bring slowly to the boil. See that the bird is clean, and free from feather scraps and pens, and put it in the liquid. Simmer gently three to four hours, according to its size and age. If the resulting broth is too fat, let it cool before attempting to skim it. Reheat and add a tablespoonful of cooked rice, or cooked soup noodles to each portion, and serve with chopped parsley or chopped chives floating on top.

If the bird is not too fat and you are sure that the broth will not need skimming, the well-washed rice, or the soup noodles can be added for the last half hour of simmering.

FRICASSEE OF CHICKEN, MADE FROM THE BIRD

Take the flesh carefully from the bones and cut into small pieces. Sweat a finely-chopped small onion in 3-3½ oz butter, then blend in 1½ oz flour, the juice of half a lemon. Then let it down to the required thickness with hot broth. Season with salt, a tea-spoonful of capers, and two chopped anchovy fillets. Finally beat the yoke of an egg into 3 tablespoonfuls of cream and stir in. Bring to the boil but do not allow to continue boiling. Pour over the pieces of chicken. This is delicious served in a rice ring. Omit the anchovy if preferred.

Thick Soups

These are made in enormous variety, and some are almost a meal in themselves, particularly in south Germany, and country districts. Many of them resemble our casseroles and stews, and only the bravest appetite would tackle anything further after such a soup, except fruit, or a light sweet. In the ordinary way, the thick soups, which the Germans call 'bound' soups, resemble our 'cream of ——'. They are thickened in various ways, by using raw, grated potato, potato flour, various cereals, rice, semolina, oatflakes, sago, and, most commonly, by a mixture of flour and fat (butter or margarine) which is made in two shades, light and dark. As the German name for this—'einbrenne'—is meaningless in translation, this book will refer to it as 'thickening, light or dark'. Those familiar with French cookery will recognise it as a *roux*. It is made as follows:—

 1½ oz butter or margarine
 1½ oz white flour

The flour is stirred into the melted fat over medium heat until it is golden in colour, or over a greater heat, for a longer period until it is dark brown. Take some of the liquid that is to be thickened and add it little by little to the thickening, beating it in until the result is liquid enough to be poured back into the soup or broth. To avoid lumps, whisk the whole strongly with an open wire whisk. Bring the whole mixture to the boil, and then, over very gentle heat, allow to simmer for not more than ten minutes.

It is important to remember that all the various thickenings for soups, stews, braised dishes, or fruit juices, are left until the last ten minutes before serving.

LEEK SOUP

2–4 leeks (*according to size*)
1½ oz butter or margarine
2 heaped tablespoonfuls flour
1½ pints water (*clear broth if you have it*)
Salt to taste
Nutmeg (*optional*)

Well wash the leeks, being careful to wash away all grit. Cut them into thin slices and sweat gently in the butter. Sprinkle the flour in gradually, keeping stirred, and fry until golden. Add the water or broth and cook gently for thirty-five to forty minutes. Season to taste with salt, and nutmeg, and at the last minute. add 2 tablespoons of cream.

If a creamlike soup is preferred, rub through a sieve and re-heat, before adding the cream.

CAULIFLOWER SOUP

1 medium sized cauliflower
1½ oz butter or margarine
2 heaped tablespoons flour
2 pints water (*preferably the water in which the cauliflower has been cooked*)

Salt

Nutmeg or lemon

1 egg yolk—or 2 tablespoons thin cream

Make a light thickening from the flour and the fat and let it down with the water in which the cauliflower has been cooked (but not overcooked). Cook this mixture gently, stirring all the time for not more than fifteen minutes, until it has thickened. Add lemon juice to taste. Stir in the well-beaten egg-yolk, or cream. Put back the cauliflower carefully, broken into rosettes. Re-heat carefully, but do not boil.

GRUEL SOUP

2½ oz mixed cereals (rice, oatflakes, groats, rolled barley)

Soup greens (be sure to include an onion)

1 oz butter

2–2½ pints milk and water (half and half)

Salt

Chopped chives or parsley

Wash the rice and barley. Dice the vegetables and add the lot to the cold, salted liquid. Boil gently for ¾ hour. Put through a fine sieve (hair or nylon). Bring again to the boil and season, adding the butter last. For a richer soup add more butter. If you use an enamel pan, make sure it is not chipped, as this may discolour your soup. If you use oatmeal, or rice flour among your cereals—mix to a smooth cream with a little of the *cold* liquid. Bring the rest of the liquid to the boil and add the creamed cereal.

TOMATO SOUP

1 lb tomatoes

1 large onion

1 small head of celery

1½ oz butter or margarine

4 level tablespoons flour

2 oz finely diced bacon or ham (smoked)

2 pints water
Salt
Pepper
1 level teaspoon sugar
3 raw tomatoes
A little unsalted butter

Cut up the pound of tomatoes and pound them to a mush. Chop the onion (peeled), cut up the celery in fine strips. Sweat the onion and celery in the butter, and when they begin to look soft add the tomato mush and fry together for a minute or two. Sprinkle the flour over the mixture and work in carefully and gradually. Add the salted water, and diced bacon or ham, and simmer gently for half an hour. Strain through a sieve, rubbing carefully, so that everything, except tomato skins and any celery fibres, goes through. Add sugar and pepper to taste. Re-heat gently and, at the last minute, add the three raw tomatoes, which have been skinned and well-mashed. This helps to restore to the soup the natural flavour of the tomatoes. A knob of fresh butter added to each serving improves the flavour.

Cheese straws or biscuits go well with this.

ONION SOUP

2 stale bread rolls
1½ oz butter or margarine
1 lb. onions
1½ oz raw smoked bacon or ham
1½ pints water (or broth—use a bouillon cube)
Salt
Pepper
¼ lb grated cheese (Parmesan will do—but you will achieve a more truly German flavour by using Gruyère or Emmenthaler that has gone hard enough to grate)

Dice the rolls and fry till golden brown in the fat. Chop the onion finely, dice the bacon, and sweat together until golden. Add the salted liquid and boil together for 30 minutes. Put the fried bread into a heated fireproof dish and pour the soup over it.

Sprinkle the cheese on top and put under a very fast grill until the surface is golden brown.

SPINACH SOUP

$\frac{1}{2}$ lb spinach
1 small onion
1 oz butter or margarine
3 oz smoked bacon
4 level tablespoons flour
1$\frac{1}{2}$ pints water (or clear broth)
Salt
2$\frac{1}{2}$ oz grated cheese (preferably Gruyère, or Emmenthaler)

Put the spinach and the onion through the mincer and sweat together in the butter. Dice the bacon, fry gently, and then sprinkle the flour gradually, continually to fry until golden. Add the water or broth and then the spinach and onion. Cook for about ten minutes after the mixture begins to simmer. Season with salt, and sprinkle with cheese after serving. If preferred, leave off the grated cheese, and serve cheese biscuits, or cheese straws.

POTATO SOUP

1 large onion
1 leek
A little celery
1 lb peeled raw potatoes
1 oz pork dripping
2 pints water (or clear broth or bouillon)
Salt and pepper
Chopped herbs
2 small bread rolls
2 oz raw smoked bacon

Chop leek, onion, and celery (after well washing) in small pieces. Fry in the fat, and add the liquid. Slice the potatoes thinly, or dice them if preferred, and boil for 10 minutes in the liquid. Rub the lot through a sieve and season with salt and pepper. Fry the diced, stale rolls in the finely-chopped bacon, and add to the soup when serving. Sprinkle with chopped herbs (parsley, chives, marjoram).

KIDNEY SOUP

2 calf's kidneys
A good oz of pork dripping
1 small onion
1 leek
1 grated carrot
½ head of celery
1 root of parsley
½ a large onion
3 level tablespoons flour
2 pints water
2 small, raw, peeled potatoes
Salt
1 egg yolk

Wash and skin the kidneys. Scald them very quickly, and then chop finely. Fry them in the fat with the chopped onion, together with all the other vegetables, also chopped. Sprinkle with the flour and gradually work it in, while still frying. Add the liquid and cook gently for thirty minutes after it comes to the simmer. In the last eight minutes, add the raw potato, shredded. Season with salt, and at the last, stir in the well-beaten egg yolk.

LIVER SOUP

1 thick slice smoked streaky bacon
¼ lb finely-chopped ox-liver
1 small onion
¾ pint clear meat broth, or vegetable broth
Salt
A little marjoram
Knob of unsalted butter

Dice the bacon and fry. Add the liver and shredded onion, and fry together, stirring to prevent sticking. Add the liquid and boil all together for five minutes. Season with salt and marjoram. Add the butter just before serving.

This soup is usually reinforced by one of the dumplings dealt with on *Garnishes and Additions for Soups*.

SOUP WITH HAM DUMPLINGS

This is an excellent way of using up stale rolls and leftover ham.

    4 *stale rolls*
    1 *gill milk*
    1 *teaspoonful finely shredded onion*
    1 *teaspoonful finely chopped parsley*
    Salt
    2 *eggs*
    3–5 *oz ham scraps (or smoked bacon)*
    Breadcrumbs
    3–4 *pints clear soup or bouillon*

Slice the rolls thinly, pour the lukewarm milk over them and leave until soft. Then mix well with well-beaten eggs, chopped onion, parsley and finely chopped ham, and season with salt. Form into little round balls, using the breadcrumbs as stiffeners, if needed. Try one in the boiling soup, to make sure that the dumpling mixture is of the right consistency, and does not fall apart. Then form the whole mass into dumplings, and cook gently in the soup for fifteen minutes. At the end of that time, lift one out and pull it apart with two forks to see if it is done.

FISH AND POTATO SOUP

    2 *pints fish stock*
    8–10 *medium sized potatoes*
    1 *onion*
    1½ *oz butter*
    8 *tablespoonfuls milk*

Salt
1 tablespoonful chopped parsley
Soup greens as available (celery, 1 grated carrot, 1 leek)
A little white wine

To make the fish stock boil bones, head (first remove the eyes) and fish scraps in the water, with plenty of the vegetables, peeled and cut up, for half an hour after coming to the boil. Peel the potatoes, cut into small dice, and fry in a little fat. Then add them to the fish and vegetable mixture and cook in it until the potatoes are soft. Rub through a sieve. Cut the onion into rings and fry in the rest of the fat. When soft, add them to the soup together with the milk. Re-heat, flavour with herbs and white wine, and sprinkle each serving with finely chopped parsley. This is a good way of using up remains of cold fish.

BEER SOUP

¾ pint light ale
¾ pint water
1½ oz sugar
3 level tablespoonfuls cornflour
Rind of half a lemon
1 egg yolk

Bring the water, sugar and lemon rind to the boil. Mix the corn-flour with a little cold water to a thin cream and stir into the boiling water. Add the beer a very little at a time, and, stirring all the time, bring to the boil again. Remove the lemon rind and thicken with the well-beaten egg yolk. This soup is good hot or cold.

Garnishes and additions for soups

Many of these have names that are unknown in English, and therefore untranslatable. Batter drops are easy, but how to deal with *klösschen* which are tiny dumpling, or *spätzle*, which are tiny strips of a dough-like batter, or *Käsestich* which are cheese-flavoured shreds? So I have done the best I can, and given the German names with an attempt at translation in each case.

BATTER DROPS

Make a very thin batter, using one egg, $\frac{1}{2}$ pint milk and water, a pinch of salt and a tablespoonful of white flour, beat this all together, as for an English Yorkshire pudding, so that the batter can be dropped, one drop at a time, from the end of a spoon. If too loose, add a little more flour. Have the soup ready boiling in its pan, and drop the batter into the boiling fluid. To speed up the process, use a colander, or grater, provided they have large holes the size of a pea, through which multiple drops of batter can be forced. When they are all in the liquid, let it stand on a very low heat for a minute or so, to allow the batter to finish cooking.

Alternatively, this same mixture can be forced through a colander, or draining spoon into boiling fat. Remove from the fat, as soon as they are golden, using a draining spoon, and drop into the soup, just before serving.

KÄSESTICH (Cheese shreds)

1 oz butter or margarine
1 oz grated Gruyère, or Emmenthaler cheese
1 egg yolk
1 teaspoonful flour

Well beat all these ingredients together as if for a cake sponge finally folding in the stiffly beaten egg white. Put the whole on a well-buttered plate, cover it tightly and cook over a pan of boiling water until the mixture sets. Cut into fine strips and set them floating in the hot soup.

WIENER ERBSEN (Viennese peas)

3 oz flour
1 egg
Pinch of salt
A few tablespoonfuls milk

Beat all this into a very stiff batter. Stir it through a large-holed colander, or draining spoon, so that bits fall into boiling fat, where they will at once take on the form of little peas. Cook until golden, and add to each serving of soup at the table.

KLÖSSCHEN (Tiny dumplings)

2½ oz butter or margarine, or (best of all) marrow fat
About ½ pint milk
6 oz flour

1 egg
Salt
Nutmeg

Boil the fat, salt and nutmeg in the milk. Tip in the flour all at once, removing pan from heat, and stir well, until the lump no longer sticks to the pot or pan. Stir the egg yolk into the hot mixture, and keep on stirring and blending until it cools. Then fold in the stiffly-beaten egg whites. Using two spoons, form into little balls, and cook for five minutes in the gently simmering soup.

LIVER KLÖSSCHEN

5 oz ox or chicken liver
2½ oz bacon
2 small onions
5 oz white flour
2 egg yolks
Salt

Put the liver, bacon and onion twice through the mincer. Stir in the beaten egg yolks and the flour. Form into little balls and drop into the gently boiling soup. After eight to ten minutes they should be done.

MEAT DUMPLINGS

2 oz butter or margarine
4 oz minced raw meat (beef, pork or veal)
2 egg yolks
2½ oz white flour
Salt
Pepper

Cream the fat until it is light and fluffy. Add the meat, flour and seasoning and bind with the well-beaten egg yolks. Form the mixture into little dumplings; put into boiling, salted water and allow to boil for at least ten minutes before you take one out and try it. When you are satisfied that the dumplings are cooked, take them out, using a draining-spoon, and set them floating in the hot soup.

Cold Fruit Soups

These are served hot or cold, according to the weather, and make an unusual, and very pleasant beginning to a rich meal, where the main dish is fried, or rather greasy. They are made in an infinite variety, using all kinds of fruit, including dried fruit. Here are a few.

BLACK CURRANT SOUP

1 *lb black currants*
1½ *pints buttermilk*
Sugar and vanilla sugar to taste

Wash the berries and take them off the stalks. Sprinkle sugar over them and leave to stand while you whisk the buttermilk until it is foamy. Stir in the berries, and sweeten to taste.

Another method. Simmer the berries gently in a very little water until the skins are soft, and then rub through a sieve. Sweeten the mush, and allow to cool, before stirring it into the beaten buttermilk. Sweeten to taste.

GOOSEBERRY COLD SOUP

1 *lb gooseberries*
1½ *pints water*
1 *heaped tablespoonful cornflour*
A little lemon rind
Sugar to taste

Wash, and top and tail the gooseberries, and simmer with the lemon rind in the water until soft. Mix the cornflour to a thin paste with a little cold water, and stir it into the berries. Bring to the boil once more, stirring well. Rub through a sieve and sweeten to taste.

BLACKBERRY COLD SOUP

1 *lb blackberries*
1 *pint water*
1 *heaped tablespoonful cornflour*
½ *pint apple juice (or cider)*

Set aside about a third of the blackberries, letting them stand with sugar sprinkled over them. Using the same method as above for gooseberries, but omitting the lemon peel, make the rest into soup. Then add the apple juice or cider. Allow to cool and pour over the sugared raw blackberries before serving. If you use bought, cultivated blackberries, remember that they are naturally much sweeter than the hedgerow fruit, and will need much less sugar, if indeed they need any.

This method can be used with any soft fruit, adding lemon juice if the fruit is naturally very sweet, or very ripe.

Fish

German housewives set a high value on fish for being rich in phosphorus and calcium, and various vitamins, and for being easily digestible, but they insist on freshness.

Sea fish is bought immediately before cooking, and freshwater fish is bought alive and killed by a smart blow on the head. If you are squeamish the fishmonger will do this for you.

If it is quite impossible for you to cook the fish as soon as you bring it home, wrap it in a cloth moistened with vinegar and stand it in a cool place in an earthenware dish. This is better than putting it in the refrigerator, which tends to spoil the flavour of the sea, which is the main attraction of really fresh fish.

Almost invariably sea fish is well sprinkled with vinegar, or lemon juice and left to stand for half an hour before cooking. This firms and whitens the flesh, and helps to preserve the flavour and smell of the sea. Fish is not salted until immediately before cooking, for the salt, if left to stand, draws out and wastes the essential juices.

Scales are removed by scraping from tail to head under a running tap, using either a knife, or a scaling brush. If they are very tough and hard to remove, dip for a split second in boiling water. Fish trimmings and heads are never thrown away, but very carefully cleaned (always throw away the eyes) and gently simmered over a slow heat, with onion, and any other root vegetables that are available, to make a nourishing broth, in which to boil fish.

It is as well to remember that, with boiled and steamed fish, however well you drain it, some further liquid will always seep into the dish. Accordingly, when making a thick sauce allow for this extra liquid by making the sauce thicker. Remember that lemon juice takes the smell of raw fish from hands very quickly.

BLUE TROUT

Anyone who has visited Germany and Austria will probably have enjoyed the famous blue trout from the mountain streams—*Forellen blau* is a familiar sign in restaurant windows, but perhaps not everyone knows that other fresh-water fish, and even herrings can also be cooked 'blue'. The fish must be freshly caught, so this method is mostly for anglers' wives.

See that your hands are wet before handling the fish, and lay it in a wet dish. It is important not to damage the natural film of slime. Do not scale the fish, but rinse it gently under a running tap. Lay it carefully in an earthenware dish, and pour over it boiling vinegar and water, or lemon juice and water. Stand in a draught to cool for about fifteen minutes. The fish can then be baked, boiled, steamed or stewed gently in a fish broth, and the deep blue colour will result.

BOILED 'BLUE'

If trout, treat as above, but arrange each fish in a circle, and secure with a small wooden skewer through tail and gills. When salting fish prepared in this manner, be careful to salt only the flesh. If the fish is very thick through, halve it and salt the flesh of each half. If very small, a little salt can be put into the belly cavity. Never let salt reach the skin. It will destroy the film which gives the blue colouring.

Lift the fish out of the vinegar and water and lay it gently in luke-warm broth or fish stock. Bring it to the boil, remove the lid, and let it stand to poach fifteen or twenty minutes, according to size.

Using two fish slices, lift out carefully onto a warmed, buttered dish.

Serve with melted butter, horseradish cream, lemon slices and garnish with parsley. Plain boiled potatoes are the usual accompaniment.

STEAMED 'BLUE'

Prepare the fish as above and then steam for fifteen to twenty minutes, over gently boiling water, to which salt, and either vinegar, or white wine has been added, in the proportion of a gill of wine or vinegar to a quart of water.
Serve as above.

BAKED 'BLUE'

Prepare the fish as above and when it begins to cool, lift it out and lay it carefully on a fire-proof plate or dish, belly side down (if the fish has been cut open, flesh side down). Cover with a wet cloth, laid over a wire grill so that it does not touch the fish, and place in a hot oven for twenty to thirty minutes. Serve with horse-radish, to which a pinch of sugar, or sweetened cream has been added.

Any of the above methods can also be used on fresh herrings.

FISH STEW

1½ lbs fillets (any white fish, but cod or haddock are best)
Vinegar or lemon juice

1½ oz butter or margarine

1 medium-sized, or 2 small onions

1½ oz flour

Salt

About half a pint of liquid. This can be fish stock, or clear
vegetable soup, and it is greatly improved if a little wine
or cider is added in the last ten minutes of cooking.

Finely chopped parsley

Tomato paste

Clean the fish; sprinkle it with vinegar or lemon juice, and let
it stand for half an hour. Salt it, and, using kitchen scissors, cut
it into strips two inches long, and about half an inch thick. While
the fish is soaking, brown the finely-chopped onion in the butter.
Roll the strips of fish in flour and brown them lightly on both
sides in the onion and fat. This is not done in a frying-pan, but
in the bottom of your stew pan. Have the liquid, and any other
ingredients (tomato paste, chopped parsley) ready heated, and add
it gradually. Stir in the rest of the flour as thickening, having
first made it into a thin cream with a little cold water or milk.
Stir very carefully, so as not to break up the fish. Cover the pan
and let it simmer on a very low heat for about half an hour until
the fish is cooked. Do not let it boil.

Serve with finely-grated cheese, or, if you like it, with sour cream.

FISH SOUFFLÉ (using cooked left-overs)

1–1½ lbs cooked fish left-overs

3 stale rolls

2½ oz raw, smoked bacon (not too fat)

3 eggs

1 gill sour cream

1 teaspoonful grated onion

1 teaspoonful chopped parsley

Salt

Remove any skin and bones from the fish, and, using two forks,
tear into small pieces. Crumble the rolls (if they are very hard
put them through the mincer). Moisten with a little water to

soften the crumbs. Drain and squeeze them well and mix with the bacon that has also been through the mincer. If liked, 2½ oz of anchovy fillets and a tablespoonful of capers can be put through the mincer and mixed with the bacon and breadcrumbs. Beat up the three egg yolks and mix all the ingredients into them, adding a little salt, but stirring carefully so as not to mash the fish pieces. Finally fold in the stiffly-beaten egg whites. Put the mixture in a well-buttered soufflé-dish. Sprinkle lightly with a tablespoonful of grated cheese and a few dabs of butter. Bake in a medium oven for ¾ hour.

FISH FRICASSÉE

1½ lbs white fish
Salt
Lemon juice or vinegar

For the Sauce:
1½ oz butter or margarine
2 oz flour
¾ pint water
1 teaspoonful capers
1–2 egg yolks
1 tablespoonful white wine (or lemon juice)
2 tablespoonfuls water
Salt

Fillet the fish and skin each fillet. Salt them and sprinkle on both sides with lemon juice and leave to soak for half an hour. Dry them well, and cut into medium sized pieces.

For the sauce, melt the butter and work the flour into it, stirring over low heat until the mixture is pale gold. Add the cold water, a little at a time, beating continuously until it boils. Put in the pieces of fish and stand for about fifteen minutes on a heat so low that it barely simmers. When the fish is cooked, stir the capers into the mixture and season it with salt. Add the wine and then the well-beaten egg yolks.

Serve the mixture in a ring of rice into which chopped parsley has been mixed. Garnish with slices of tomato.

1½ *lbs fish fillets (any white fish)*
lemon juice or vinegar, salt
1 *dessertspoonful made mustard*
1 *dessertspoonful anchovy paste*

for the tomato sauce:
1½ *oz butter or margarine*
1 *small onion*
½ *lb tomatoes*
2 *oz white flour*
3 *gills water*
Salt
Lemon juice

Skin the fillets, salt them and sprinkle with lemon juice, leaving to stand for half an hour. Dry carefully and cut into strips suitable for rolling. Spread some with anchovy paste, and some with mustard. If preferred, use a mixture of finely-minced smoked bacon, cooked onion and chopped parsley. Roll each piece and secure with a cherry stick. Place all the rolls, standing on end and closely packed in a well-buttered, fireproof dish—a soufflé-dish is best. It should be flame-proof.

For the sauce: chop the peeled onions finely. slice the tomatoes and fry them lightly together in the melted butter. Stir in the flour, little by little, and then, very gradually add the water, stirring all the time, and boil for a few minutes. Put through a sieve, and then, using a fiercer heat, bring once more to the boil. Season and pour over the fish rolls. Allow to simmer very gently for ten minutes, and then, with the heat at its lowest, preferably using an asbestos mat, for another ten minutes. An alternative method of cooking is to put the rolled fillets in a buttered soufflé dish. Stir some tomato purée, or tomato paste into sour cream, pour over the fish rolls and bake in a medium oven for about forty-five minutes.

CARP WITH CREAM SAUCE

1 *oz butter or margarine*
Parsley, chervil, tarragon

1 small onion
1 gill sour cream
3 tablespoonfuls clear meat broth

Fillet the carp and carefully scrape off all the scales. Slice through each fillet once more and salt them. Melt the butter and simmer the grated onion in it gently, together with the finely chopped herbs. Add the pieces of fish and pour over them the cream and the broth. If a flame-proof dish is used, the whole operation can be carried out in the same dish, which is then transferred to a hot oven for fifteen to twenty minutes.

FILLETS OF FISH AND MACARONI

½ lb macaroni
Salt
2½ oz butter or margarine
1 lb fish fillets
Lemon juice
2 tablespoonfuls skinned and chopped mushrooms
2 tomatoes
1 small onion
2 oz grated cheese

Cook the macaroni in salted boiling water—not too soft, but 'al dente' as the Italians say. Drain it, and using two forks, toss it in half of the butter. Lay it in a fireproof dish which has been well-buttered. Season the fish fillets, and after letting them stand in lemon juice for half an hour, dry them carefully and lay them on the macaroni. Slice tomatoes and onions finely, and lay them on top of the fish, together with the chopped mushrooms. Sprinkle the grated cheese; add the rest of the butter in small dabs, and bake until golden brown.

MARINATED HERRINGS (salted)

Soak the herrings for at least twenty-four hours in frequent changes of cold water. Take off heads and tails. Gut and skin them carefully, making sure that you remove all scales. If very heavily salted, soak for another day in milk.

The liquid for marinating is prepared as follows:—

½ pint water
½ pint vinegar
2 or three bay leaves (bruised)
2–3 cloves
10 peppercorns
1 dessertspoonful mustard seed
One large, or two small onions, skinned and finely sliced

Boil all these ingredients together and allow to grow cold. Place the fish in a dish long enough to allow them to lie flat, pour the marinade over them. It must cover them completely. Cover the dish tightly and leave in a cool place for two or three days.

MARINATED HERRINGS (fresh)

8 fresh herrings
Flour
Fat for frying
Marinade liquid, made as above

Gut, wash and scrape the herrings, carefully removing all scales. Salt them lightly and roll in flour. Fry them on both sides in hot fat until golden-brown. As herrings are rich in oil, very little fat is needed to fry them.

Make the marinade as above; let it go cold and pour it over the still warm herrings. Closely cover the dish and stand in a cool place for two or three days.

FISH FOR A GOURMET

This method is suitable for any of the firm-fleshed, good quality fish like turbot, halibut, or even cod and fresh haddock.

The fillets (or cutlets) of fish are seasoned with salt and pepper and grilled in butter, in the usual way, and placed on a warmed dish. The sauce is made as follows:—

Finely sliced, peeled mushrooms and crab or lobster meat, finely diced are gently stewed in butter. Best is a flame-proof glass braising pan. Whisk together 1 tablespoon tomato purée, cream at your discretion, and a little cornflour for thickening. Add this to the mushroom mixture and cook very gently, stirring occasionally until the ingredients are tender. Season to taste with salt and pepper, and a little sugar. Pour over the fish and serve at once. This dish can be made even more exotic by letting the fish soak in a good marinade for half an hour before grilling.

MARINADE

1 *cup dry white wine*
½ *cup water*
1 *medium-sized onion*
sprig of parsley
2 *outside stalks of celery, with green leaves*
1 *small carrot*

Finely chop onion, parsley, celery and carrot and bring to the boil in the liquid. A sprig of rosemary, or a bay leaf can be added, but should be whipped out as soon as the mixture comes to the boil.

SOLE WITH ASPARAGUS

2 *medium-sized soles*
1 *lb asparagus*
Lemon juice
Butter
Salt
Pepper
1 *gill cream*
A little white wine

Clean and skin the soles. Steep them in lemon juice for half an hour. Dry thoroughly and salt. Fry them in butter on both sides. Boil and drain the asparagus. Place in the frying-pan with the fish, turning the asparagus in the butter until they are covered with it and hot. Whisk together thoroughly the cream and the white wine and pour over the fish and asparagus. Allow to heat up gently before serving.
Serve with a lettuce salad and boiled potatoes.

Pork

There are innumerable dishes, using every conceivable cut of pork, and a great variety of wurst (sausages) large and small, hard and soft, with and without garlic, which are contrived from pork and veal, finely minced and blended with fat, some cereal, and different flavourings. Many of these are familiar and available to those who live in our big towns, being freely on sale at delicatessen counters and in the self-service stores.

PORK STEW

Use any of the cheaper cuts, paring away excess fat.

1 lb meat
½ pint water
1½ ozs fat bacon
2 ozs flour
1 onion

1 *lb cooking apples*
1–2 *tablespoonfuls vinegar, or lemon juice*
4–6 *ozs dried fruit (sultanas or raisins)*
Sugar
Salt

Cut the meat in pieces as for a beef stew and put it in salted boiling water, letting it simmer on a gentle heat for about an hour and a half. The dried fruit should have been well-washed and soaked in water over-night. Take away most of the liquid from the meat, and while it is cooling, bring the dried fruit to the boil in the liquid in which it has been soaking, and simmer gently for twenty minutes.

Fry the fat bacon, dicing it first, and then, over gentle heat, work in the flour, and the finely chopped onion. Cook until the mixture is golden brown. Keeping it stirred, add the cooled liquid in which you have cooked the pork, a little at a time, and bring to the boil, then, lowering your heat cook very gently until it thickens. Flavour this sauce with sugar, salt, and either vinegar or lemon juice. Put the meat, and the sultanas or raisins back into the sauce, and re-heat gently before serving.

Make a purée of the apples, as follows. Peel, core, and slice into small pieces. Use a thick-bottomed saucepan, into which you have put about two tablespoons of cold water. Stir constantly until the fruit falls into a purée. Then sweeten, if they need it. A good cooking-apple (Bramley, or Derby or Keswick) takes no more than five or six minutes.

Serve with boiled potatoes, or, if the weather is very cold, with dumplings, made as shown on *Dumplings*. The purée is served separately, as a garnish.

This same method is also used with beef, lamb, or veal, but rather more onion is added and a bay leaf, or sprig of basil, and a leaf of lovage, if available.

BRAISED PORK CUTLETS

4 *small pork cutlets*
Flour

Salt
Pepper
Paprika
2 garlic cloves
2 onions
1½ ozs fat (preferably pork dripping)
1 green pepper
2½ ozs raw smoked bacon (not too fat)
4 tomatoes
1 cup sour cream

Cut away surplus fat from the cutlets. If there is enough, melt it down and use for frying them. Season them with pepper and salt, and roll well in a mixture of flour and paprika. (A teaspoonful of paprika to two tablespoons of flour should be enough.) Fry them in the fat over a strong heat till both sides are well-browned. Cut up the bacon, and the green pepper into slivers, using kitchen scissors, and chop the onions finely.

Put the cutlets into a glass casserole, arranging the onion, bacon, crushed garlic and pepper around and over them. Pour over them the fat in which they were fried, and braise slowly in a medium oven for about 45 minutes. When the meat is nearly done, add the tomatoes, skinned and sliced and put back for another fifteen to twenty minutes. When you are satisfied that the meat is tender, lift it out, skim off any excess fat, and stir in the sour cream. Re-heat in the oven, and pour over the cutlets which have been kept hot on the serving dish. This dish is just as tasty without the garlic. If you have a flame-proof casserole the whole dish can be cooked on the boiling ring or plate, using an asbestos mat to slow it down, if necessary. A heavy-bottomed saucepan can also be used.

BRAISED PORK FILLET

1 pork fillet (about one pound)
1 oz of fat bacon (for frying. Butter or margarine can be used)
1 onion
1 large tomato

Salt
Pepper
Flour
Water
Sour cream or buttermilk

Skin the fillet and remove any gristle. Rub well with pepper and salt, and fry both sides in the hot fat, adding the chopped onion, and the tomato (skinned and cut up small), until golden brown. If the tomato is very watery, no more liquid is needed, but if not, add a very little water. Cover the pan and braise for about twenty minutes—do not over-cook. Keep the meat warm while the sauce is prepared, by stirring the flour gently over low heat into the sour cream, or milk, adding a knob of butter, as desired, and seasoning with salt and pepper. Pour over the pork fillet, and serve. Any young vegetables, peas, French beans, asparagus, go well with this dish.

BRAISED PORK

1–1½ *lbs lean pork meat (shoulder or leg)*
1–1½ *oz fat (preferably pork or bacon fat)*
1–2 *teaspoonfuls flour*
1 *small onion*
Stewing vegetables as desired (leek, celery, turnip, carrot etc.)
Sprig of basil
Salt
Cream
1 *pint liquid (bouillon, or the liquid in which the vegetables have been cooked)*

The meat can be cut up, as for a stew, or braised in a lump. Rub it with salt. Brown it all over on a fast heat in the fat. Add the vegetables and onion, all cut up finely, and allow them to simmer gently for a few minutes, while the liquid is heating in another pan. Then add the heated liquid gradually, stirring in carefully. Lower the heat, and allow to simmer gently in a tightly-covered pan for one to two hours, trying the meat from time to time, until it is tender. Add the basil, and, if obtainable, one leaf of lovage, when the meat is within half an hour of being cooked. Finally stir in the flour to thicken.

Two to three tablespoons of cream are a great improvement.

PORK SCHNITZEL OR ESCALOPE

Allow one slice per person
Salt
Pepper
Flour and a little milk, or 1 egg and dried breadcrumbs
Fat for frying, preferably pork dripping or lard.

Beat the slices well on both sides. Rub with pepper and salt. Dip each in beaten egg and then breadcrumbs, or if preferred, in milk and then flour, and fry golden-brown in hot fat. Garnish with slices of lemon, anchovy fillets and capers.

BAKED TITBIT

4 thin pork slices
Fat for frying (preferably pork fat)
Salt
Pepper
Nutmeg
Butter
About 2 oz mushrooms
3 eggs
2 tablespoonfuls flour
2 tablespoonfuls grated cheese
1½ lbs asparagus
Butter flakes

Rub the pork slices with salt and fry them on both sides. Cut the peeled mushrooms into fine slices, mix with the cooked and drained asparagus, which is also cut into short lengths, and season with salt, pepper, and a little grated nutmeg. Put this mixture with the fried pork slices into a buttered, fire-proof casserole. Whisk the eggs and pour over. Sprinkle the flour and cheese on top and dot little flakes of butter all over the surface.

Bake in a fast oven until nicely browned, about twenty minutes.
Serve with lettuce salad with a sharp dressing, and mashed potatoes.

PORK GOULASH WITH PAPRIKA

1½ lbs lean pork meat, cut up into medium pieces
3 onions
2 tomatoes
2 pickled gherkins
Fat for frying (butter or pork fat)
Flour
Paprika
Water

Rub the pork with salt and fry in hot fat till golden-brown on
all sides. Then add the diced, skinned tomatoes, diced onion,
and finely chopped gherkin, and let all cook together until the
onion is golden-brown. This should take about fifteen minutes.
Sprinkle freely with flour and half a teaspoon of paprika. Add a
little hot water, cover tightly and leave to simmer on a gentle
heat, for about half an hour. Add water from time to time, to
keep the meat half-covered. When cooked, stir in a little cream
or, if preferred, a little tomato purée.

PIGS' KIDNEYS—SWEET-SOUR

4 kidneys
Fat for frying
Salt
Pepper
Flour
Water
2 onions
Sugar
Wine or vinegar

Skin the kidneys. Slit them longways, and remove the white
tendons. Scald them very briefly, and cut into strips.
Brown the strips very quickly in very hot fat, and add the diced

onions. Season with salt and pepper and sprinkle freely with flour. Add as much water as you want gravy, cover, and boil for five minutes. Add caster sugar and white wine, or vinegar, until the sweet sour effect is achieved. This entire dish should be prepared as quickly as possible, with the minimum of cooking, so as not to make the kidneys hard.

PORK ROLLS

1 lb of lean pork meat
2 ozs smoked, streaky bacon
2 onions
2 oz fat for frying
Fat for frying
Salt
Parsley
1 tablespoonful flour
½ pint liquid (water or meat broth. Use a bouillon cube)
Soup vegetables as desired (celery, leek, carrot, etc.)

Cut the meat into slices about half an inch thick, and beat well with rolling-pin until flat. Rub with salt. Put the bacon, one of the onions, and the parsley through the mincer, and fry lightly, stirring to prevent sticking. Spread this mixture on the pork slices. Roll up, and secure with a cherry stick, or tie lightly with fine string. Roll them in flour and brown all over in very hot fat. Add the second onion, peeled and chopped, and the finely-diced vegetables, and brown them all with the meat rolls. Add the warmed liquid gradually, cover the pan, and simmer until tender for one to one and a half hours.

If desired, a little sour milk or cream can be stirred in at the last moment before serving.

PORK FILLET IN PASTRY

Take a nice juicy fillet. Skin it, rub lightly with salt and paprika, and brown quickly all over in very hot butter. It is a good idea to put a small sprig of rosemary, or one or two leaves of sage in the butter. When browned all over, lift out the fillet and leave it to cool. Then roll it in short, or flaky pastry and seal it carefully in. Prick the pastry on top and brush with yolk of egg. Bake in a pre-heated oven for about thirty minutes until brown and crisp.

BELLY OF PORK WITH SWEDE TURNIPS

1½ lbs swedes
1 lb fresh belly of pork
1 oz fat
1½ lbs potatoes
Flour
Salt
Water

Peel the swedes, and flake with the point of a sharp knife. Peel and dice the potatoes, and put with the swedes, salt, and a little water, into a covered dish or casserole. Lay the pork on top, and allow to braise slowly in a moderate oven. When cooked, take out the meat, and keep it hot. Work the flour into the fat, over heat until nut-brown. Stir this thickening into the vegetables and heat until thickened. Slice the pork, lay the slices on top and serve. The pork can be seasoned in various ways, before cooking. Salt, and a little paprika, salt, and a few pinches of finely rubbed herbs can be rubbed into it, or it can be slit and the seasoning inserted.

Dumplings go well with this. See *Dumplings and Boiled Puddings*.

GRIEBEN

These are the crisp brown fragments of fat left from the rendering down of pork, beef, suet and even goose and duck fat. The raw fat is put through a mincer so that the remains are small and crumb-like. In South Germany, and in cold, mountain districts generally, they are eaten in various ways, mixed with boiled, sliced potatoes, finely chopped onion, and either fried, or baked in the oven.

In Bavaria they mix pork 'grieben', sliced apple and onion rings and bake them in a shallow dish. The result is then used as a filling for pastries, or spread on bread. It is also very useful with bacon. If you ever make a bacon flan, try adding some.

Veal

Veal is, if possible, even more popular than pork, and is also of first class quality. Any of the recipes given in the previous section on Pork, are equally successful with veal except that the clever cook will vary her flavourings according to her own tastes, remembering that the delicate flavour of the meat itself needs more careful seasoning, so as not to be lost. Remember also that veal shrinks considerably during cooking. It is not so nourishing as beef and is a dish for adults, rather than for growing children. However, if your children love a veal schnitzel and continually ask for it, put a fried egg on top of each slice just before serving. This will make up the lack of goodness. The Germans and Austrians invariably serve a fresh, green salad with a sharp dressing, as an accompaniment to any schnitzel, to counter-balance its richness.

4 thin slices of veal
1 egg
Flour
Breadcrumbs
Salt
Pepper
Lemon
Parsley
Butter to fry

Well beat the slices between greaseproof paper, unless the butcher has already done this for you. See that each is dry. Add a little water to the egg when beating it. Dip each slice into flour, after rubbing it with salt. Then dip in the beaten egg, and finally in breadcrumbs. Fry 10–15 minutes in hot, melted butter. Garnish with a slice of lemon and a few capers, or a tablespoon of chopped, hard-boiled egg.

VEAL SCHNITZEL IN FOIL

Choose very lean veal. Spread the foil with butter, and sprinkle a little curry-powder on it, or, if preferred, a little paprika powder. Rub the meat with salt and wrap up securely. It is best to do each slice in its own separate jacket of foil. Bake in a medium oven until tender. Serve with a lettuce salad made with a lemon juice dressing.

BAVARIAN SCHNITZEL

The veal slices, beaten very thin, are spread with sausage-meat. Ordinary, good quality pork sausage meat, with a little rubbed sage and grated onion added, and bound with beaten yolk of egg is best. Roll up the slices and secure at each end with two brochette pins. Dunk them in cooking oil, or melted butter (the latter gives a better flavour) and grill gently for 5 to 10 minutes, turning continuously. You can save all the juice if you wrap each roll in foil, and you can also tie them with fine twine, instead of the brochette pins, but you will need a hotter grill. Turn out on to very hot plates, season, pour the juice and extra melted butter over them, and sprinkle with finely chopped parsley. Serve with plain boiled potatoes, lemon slices and a salad with lemon juice dressing.

FRICASSÉE OF VEAL IN A RICE RING

1 lb veal
2 oz butter
1 egg yolk
½ pint liquid
1 teaspoonful capers
Flour
Salt
Lemon juice
2–3 ozs button mushrooms

Cut up the meat in pieces about the size of half a crown and boil gently in salted water until tender. Work the flour into the butter over low heat until pale gold and then stir in gradually ½ pint of the liquid in which the meat has cooked. If there is still any liquid left from the meat, use it to stew gently, for about five minutes the diced and peeled mushrooms. If there is no liquid left, use a very little milk. Season the sauce with capers, lemon juice and salt, but do not let it boil again. Cut the meat into dice, or halve each piece, which is quicker, and add it, with the mushrooms to the sauce. Re-heat, but do not allow to boil, and serve in the middle of a ring of hot, buttered rice, which has been freely sprinkled with chopped parsley.

VEAL WITH TOMATOES

1 lb lean veal
2 oz butter or margarine
½ lb tomatoes (some cooks use a whole pound)
2–3 onions (according to size)
6 oz rice

Salt
Curry powder
1 pint water
1 gill sour cream
2 ozs mushrooms

Cut the meat into small pieces, sprinkle with salt, and lightly brown in the melted butter, turning it constantly with a fork. Shortly before it is brown enough, add the peeled and chopped mushrooms, the peeled and diced onion and the skinned and sliced tomatoes, and keep well stirred, allowing all the ingredients to blend without sticking. Add the water, raise the heat, and bring the mixture up to boiling point. Then lower the heat and allow to simmer gently for about twenty-five minutes. Well wash and drain the rice, and add to the rest. Bring again to the boil, and then simmer again on a low light until the rice is cooked. Season with salt. The cream goes in ten minutes before serving: and so does the curry powder, if used.

VEAL AND ASPARAGUS RICE

½ lb lean veal
1 lb asparagus
1 onion
2 cups rice
4 cups water
2 tablespoonfuls oil (or melted butter)
3 ozs butter

Salt
Curry powder
Parsley

Sweat the finely diced onion in the oil (or melted butter). Wash and dry the rice, and fry it with the onion until golden. Add the water and let it cook gently for twenty minutes, until all the water is absorbed. Season with salt and curry powder, and keep warm. Cut the veal into match strips, sprinkle with salt and fry in hot butter until tender. Arrange the veal, and cooked and drained asparagus in the bottom of a serving dish, and put the rice on top. Pour a little melted butter over it and garnish with the parsley.

Beef

Always see that whatever cut you buy, it has been well hung. Meat that is too new is invariably tough, even though it may be of good quality, and from a young animal. Recipes using vinegar or wine, or beer, are useful for tenderising meat which you suspect is going to be tough and stringy. Beef bought in a German butcher's shop is usually much leaner than ours, and most recipes are for lean meat that needs the addition of some fat to help make it tender.

BEEF SOUR

    1½–2 lbs beef (any lean cut)
    Buttermilk (or marinade liquid)
    Root vegetables as desired
    1 oz fat bacon
    2 ozs butter
    Salt

For the marinade:

    1 *onion*
    ½ *pint water*
    1 *gill vinegar*
    5 *peppercorns*
    1 *clove*
    A small bay leaf
    ½ *teaspoonful mixed spice*

Boil together all the ingredients for the marinade, slicing the onion finely, and allow to cool. Pour over the raw meat and allow to stand in a covered dish, in a cool place, for two to three days. Before cooking, take it out, and dry it very carefully.

Dice the bacon, and fry it in the butter. Take out the bacon bits (do not throw them away) and brown the meat (which has been rubbed with salt) all over in the hot fat. Then add the vegetables, cut up small, and fry together for a few minutes. Then add hot water, or, better, beef broth, or bouillon, so that three-quarters of the meat is covered. Put back the fried bacon bits. Cover the pan and braise slowly for 1½ hours, or thereabouts, turning frequently. If desired, some of the strained marinade liquor can be added for flavouring. When the meat is tender, thicken the liquid with a little cornflour. Sour cream, added at the last minute, is an extra touch of luxury, if you happen to like it.

BOILED BEEF WITH MUSTARD SAUCE

    1–1½ *lbs beef*
    1 *large onion*
    Choice of root vegetables (carrot, turnip, celery, parsnip, leek etc.)
    Water
    Salt

Beat the meat gently with a rolling-pin. Put it into boiling salted water, with the onion, which has been peeled and quartered. Bring to the boil again and, in a closely-covered pan, simmer for two hours. During the last hour add the vegetables, cut up very small. When the meat is tender, remove the heat, and leave standing in the liquid for ten minutes, while you make the sauce.

Using some of the liquid, make a mustard sauce as follows:—
Melt a knob of butter (1–1½ ozs) in the bottom of a saucepan
and work in white flour until thick and pale golden. Little by
little stir in ½–¾ pint of the liquid, keeping it boiling as you stir,
and then let it stand for five minutes. Finally add two tablespoons of powdered mustard, a pinch of sugar, and a little vinegar.
Bring to the boil again, and serve, ladling it over the sliced beef.

BEEF ROLLS

4 *thin slices of meat* (*topside is good*)
1 *onion*
2 *ozs butter, or pork fat*
Flour
2 *ozs smoked bacon*
Water or bouillon
Flour or cornflour for the sauce

Well beat the meat slices on both sides. Salt and pepper them and
sprinkle sparsely with mustard powder. Spread each slice with
chopped onion (if you like a lot of onion, you will need more
than the one indicated) and three narrow strips of the bacon.
Roll up, and tie, or secure with a cocktail stick. Dredge flour
over them, and brown on all sides in hot fat, in which a little
chopped onion has been fried. Add the hot water or bouillon
and braise slowly, in a covered pan for about an hour.
Flavour with tomato paste, or paprika, or sour cream.

VIENNA STEAKS WITH EGG

1 *lb of lean beef*
2 *onions*
1 *bread roll—soaked in milk or water, and squeezed dry*
2 *ozs smoked bacon*
2 *hard-boiled eggs*
1 *egg* (*raw*)
About 1 oz (*scant*) *flour*

Salt

Pepper

Paprika

Put the meat through the mincer. Cut the bacon into dice, and mix half of it with the bread roll (which has been broken up with two forks), the salt, paprika and pepper into the minced meat, binding the mixture with the well-beaten egg. Form the mixture into a long, pasty-like roll, round the shelled, hard-boiled eggs, which lie, side by side in the middle. Cut the rest of the bacon into thin strips and lay them on the upper surface of the roll, pressing gently into position. If liked, use more bacon, and lace the whole of the upper surface with strips.

Bake in a hot oven, and thicken the gravy which comes out with flour, pouring it over the roll before carving.

BEEF CASSEROLE WITH TOMATOES, BEANS AND POTATOES

1 lb beef. (*Choose a cut well-marbled with fat*)

1 oz fat

1 lb tomatoes

1½ lbs potatoes

1½ lbs green kidney beans

1 gill liquid

3 onions

2 ozs bacon

Salt

Paprika

Parsley

Cut the meat into dice and lightly brown in the fat. Arrange layers in the casserole as follows:— first a layer of beans, tomatoes and onions cut up small, then a layer of meat, then a layer of diced potatoes, then diced bacon. Then begin again, ending with bacon on the top. Add the liquid. Sprinkle the surface with flour and paprika and a few chopped herbs if you like them. Stew gently in the casserole in a moderate oven until done. Garnish with chopped fresh parsley.

(This is a famous German stew, using mixed meats, and is an excellent cold weather dish.)

    1 lb mixed meats (*beef, pork, veal, and lamb or mutton*)
    1½ lbs mixed root vegetables (*with celery and leeks if available*)
    1 *large onion*
    One or two cabbage leaves
    3–4 ozs marrow fat (*if you can't get it, use beef suet*)
    1 lb potatoes
    Meat bouillon
    Salt

This dish needs a casserole with a tightly fitting lid to keep in essential juices. Cut half the marrow-fat, or suet into slices, and lay them on the bottom of the casserole. Then add in layers, the meat, diced and salted, the chopped onion, the diced potatoes and the sliced vegetables (except the cabbage leaves). Finally, on top, spread the cabbage leaves, broken into small pieces. Add enough liquid (meat bouillon) to half-fill the vessel, and lastly, resting on the cabbage leaves, slices of the rest of the marrow-fat or suet. Cover tightly, and braise in a moderate to slow oven for about 1½ to 2 hours, shaking well from time to time.

CASSEROLE WITH CARROTS

    1 lb beef
    1 lb carrots
    3 tomatoes
    2 onions
    1½ lbs potatoes
    1 oz flour
    Water
    A little milk
    Salt
    Pepper
    Chopped parsley

Dice the meat, and partly cook in salted water with the chopped onions. Cut the carrots into flakes, using the point of a short, sharp knife. Cut the peeled potatoes into thick slices. Put meat, and vegetables, with sprinklings of salt and pepper, in layers in a casserole, or covered dish. Braise slowly, in a medium to slow oven. After an hour, add the tomatoes, skinned and sliced, and return to the oven. Lastly stir the flour into a thin paste in a little milk, and stir this into the casserole. When it has thickened it is ready to serve. Sprinkle with chopped parsley.

KÖNIGSBERGER KLOPS (Meat Balls)

1 *lb beef mince (or beef and pork mixed)*
1 *egg*
1 *oz (good measure) fat*
1 *onion*
1 *oz flour*
1 *bread roll (that has been soaked in milk or water, and squeezed or pressed dry)*
2 *tablespoonfuls capers*
Salt
Pepper
Vinegar or wine
3 *gills of meat bouillon*
1 *salted herring (if preferred, this can be omitted)*

Grate the onion. Break up the roll, and work it, with the onion, salt and pepper, into the minced meat, binding the lot with the well-beaten egg. If the herring is used, skin and bone it and work the mashed flesh into the mixture. Form into small dumplings. Melt the fat and work the flour into it over heat, until golden-brown. Add the bouillon little by little, stirring thoroughly and continually, and bring it to the boil. Lower the heat, and when the liquid is simmering gently put in the meat balls, and let them cook over low heat for fifteen to twenty minutes.

When finished flavour the liquid with either vinegar or wine, and add the capers.

Lamb and Mutton

After beef, mutton is regarded as being the most nourishing of the meats, but the German housewife insists on its being well hung. Mutton fat is considered to be very difficult to digest and so is entirely removed before cooking. All the following recipes, therefore, assume that very lean meat is being used.

STEWED LAMB

1 *lb lamb or mutton (neck end or stewing lamb)*
2 *tablespoonfuls tomato purée or pulp*
1 *onion*
4 *shallots*
1 *oz flour*
Fat for frying
Water or meat bouillon

Salt

A sprinkle of paprika

If you like garlic, use garlic salt, which gives a faint aroma of garlic

Trim the meat, remove any loose bits of bone and cut into pieces. If you have time, take scrag or neck end off the bone, using a very sharp knife, but simmer the bones in a separate pan, with a little salt, and a very small sprig of rosemary, and use the resulting stock instead of the meat bouillon.

Rub the pieces of meat with salt, and one garlic clove, finely chopped (or use garlic salt), dust them with paprika, and fry quickly on both sides, in very hot fat. Stir in the tomato pulp while frying. Set aside, while you sweat in butter, the finely-chopped onion and shallots until golden brown. Add these to the meat and tomato. Add enough stock or meat bouillon to float, but not to cover the meat. Sprinkle fairly thickly with flour, cover the pan, and allow to braise slowly for forty-five minutes to one hour.

BRAISED MUTTON

This method can turn rather tough old meat into a very tasty dish like venison or game.

1 lb meat, in a piece

3 onions

½ garlic clove

1 teaspoonful carraway seeds, or if preferred 3 or 4 juniper berries

Fat for frying

Water

Flour for thickening

Buttermilk. If this is not available, make a marinade.

Cut away all superfluous fat. Steep the meat for two or three days either in buttermilk, or a cold marinade. Dry the meat carefully, and rub with salt and paprika. Brown on all sides in a heavy-bottomed pan, or flame-proof casserole. Add the peeled and diced onions, the garlic, and the carraway (or juniper). Fry all together for a few minutes. Then add liquid, according to the amount of gravy you will need. Cover closely, and braise slowly over low heat, turning the meat over from time to time, until it is tender. Lift out the meat, and stir flour into the gravy to thicken.

CASSEROLE OF MUTTON WITH BEANS AND TOMATOES

  1 *lb lamb or mutton*
  1 *onion*
  ½ *lb tomatoes*
  1 *lb green beans*
  1 *lb potatoes*
  1 *gill stock*
  Salt

Bone the meat, and simmer the bones to make a little stock. Fry the salted meat on both sides in hot fat. Add the chopped onions, and, about five minutes later, the tomatoes, skinned and cut up finely. Continue frying this until onion and tomato are well blended. Then add the beans and potatoes, finely sliced and pour in the stock.

Cover the pan and increase the heat until steam begins to rise. Then lower the heat until no steam rises, otherwise the amount of liquid allowed will not suffice. This is a fairly solid dish, like a hotpot, and is cooked in the minimum of liquid. Do not stir, which would break up the potatoes and beans, and do not remove the lid, but leave to simmer, on very low heat, for about an hour and a half. Look in the pan after an hour to see if done.

VIENNA BRAISED CABBAGE

This recipe is inserted here, although it uses pork, because the method of preparing and cooking is exactly the same as for the mutton casserole immediately above.

  1 *lb lean pork*
  ½ *lb assorted diced carrot, turnip, leek, celery*
  1½ *lbs white cabbage*
  1 *lb potatoes*
  1 *gill stock*

Salt
Pepper
Marjoram
A little garlic (or garlic salt)
1 onion

Proceed exactly as for the Casserole of Mutton with Beans and Tomatoes.

MUTTON WITH TURNIPS

1 lb mutton or lamb (bone and simmer the bones to make stock)
1½ lbs turnips
1 lb potatoes
½ to ¾ pint stock
1 onion
Salt
Pepper

Proceed exactly as for the Casserole of Mutton with Beans and Tomatoes.

Potato Dishes

BACON POTATOES

1½ *lbs potatoes*
3 *gills stock (or meat bouillon)*
2 *ozs smoked fat bacon*
1 *onion*
A little flour
A little butter
Chopped chives

Cut the bacon into dice and fry lightly. Add the butter, the chopped onion and the flour and fry together. Peel the potatoes and dice them, and fry up for a few minutes with the onion and bacon. Then add the stock, cover, and leave to steam on the lowest possible heat until cooked. All the liquid will be soaked up. Garnish with chopped chives.

FARMHOUSE BREAKFAST

Use cold boiled potatoes, firm enough to slice. Fry a chopped onion in butter or margarine, with a little diced, smoked bacon.

Sprinkle salt on the potato slices and add them to the frying mixture, turning the slices frequently with a palette knife. Beat up an egg with a little milk, add a little diced, smoked ham and pour over the potatoes. Shake lightly over a moderate heat until the egg is set, trying not to break the potato slices. Sprinkle with chopped chives, and serve at once piping hot.

POTATO CHEESE PUDDING

1 lb cold boiled potatoes
10 ozs cheese curd
2–3 eggs
3 heaped tablespoonfuls fine semolina
6 oz diced meat leftovers, or ham
Salt
Pepper
Nutmeg

Pass the curd through a sieve. Separate egg yolks and whites. Grater the potatoes, or crumble them with a fork, according to how firm they are. Mix all the ingredients with the egg yolk. Then fold in the stiffly-beaten egg whites. Turn into a well-greased pudding bowl or soufflé dish. Boil in a bain-marie, or steam for one hour, and turn out on a warmed dish.
Serve with green salad, or a sharp sauce.

POTATO CHEESE SLICES

1 lb cold boiled potatoes
½ lb cheese curd
½ a grated onion
2 tablespoonfuls chopped parsley
1 egg
A little diced ham
Fat for frying
Salt

Grater or crumble with a fork the potatoes and, with all the other ingredients mix into a dough. Roll out into round, flat cakes, dip in egg, and fry golden brown.

POTATO PASTY

    1 *lb cold boiled potatoes*
    1 *egg*
    1 *oz flour*
    Salt

Filling:
    ¼ *lb minced meat leftovers, or ham, or smoked sausage, or mush-*
        rooms
    Onion
    Herbs
    1 *egg*
    Sour cream

Make a dough, firm enough to be rolled by breaking up the potatoes with a fork, or putting them through a 'snailer', and mixing them well with first, the flour, which is best worked in by hand, salting, and stirring in the egg. Roll and cut into thin rounds.

For the filling finely chop, or put through the mincer, onion, herbs, and the mushrooms or meat and the sour cream. Keep aside some of the egg yolk. Spread the filling on each round of the potato pastry and fold over carefully sealing the edge by means of the egg yolk. Brush over the top with the rest of the egg yolk, place on a greased tin, and bake until golden brown.

POTATO SAUSAGE ROLLS

Make a potato dough, exactly as in the preceding recipe for Potato Pasty, and roll out until a good ¼ inch thick. Cut into oblong pieces large enough to enclose the type of sausage you are using. The sausage should be boiled for a minute or two to firm it, then skinned and slit lengthways. It will taste all the better if a sprinkle of rubbed, dried sage, or marjoram, is put

between the halves. Make each sausage into a pasty, carefully
sealing the edges of the dough, using either milk or egg, and
closing both ends. Brush over with milk or egg, and bake until
golden brown on a greased tin, in a moderate to hot oven.
Serve with a green salad, or gherkins.

STUFFED POTATOES

Boil in their skins the potatoes, which should be large and even
in size. Halve them, remove some of the middle and spread a
large dab of liver-sausage in the hollow. Put the halves carefully
together again, and place in a greased soufflé dish. Bake for ten
to fifteen minutes in a hot oven.
If preferred they can be fried, browning on both sides. This
latter method is better when the potatoes are new and thin-
skinned as the skin and the outer layer of flesh will crisp up like a
roasted potato and can be eaten. Particularly delicious if fried
in pork dripping or in bacon fat.

POTATO OMELETTE

> 1 *lb potatoes*
> 1 *onion*
> 2 *oz diced, smoked bacon*
> 1 *level tablespoonful flour*
> 2 *eggs*
> 8 *tablespoonfuls milk*
> *Salt*
> *Chopped chives*
> *Parsley*

Wash the potatoes and boil them in their skins. Peel as soon as
done, and allow to cool. Fry the bacon with a little salt in a
frying-pan. Dice the onions, cut the cold potatoes into slices, and
fry with the bacon until well-browned.
Beat together the eggs, flour, milk, a little salt, the chopped parsley
and chives and pour over the mixture in the frying pan. Reduce

heat and allow the egg to set. When the under part is brown, slide the omelette onto a heated dish, folding it in the process. Serve at once.

POTATO MOULD

2–2½ lbs potatoes
2 onions
1 oz butter
1 lb mixed mince (beef and pork, or veal and pork)
1 tablespoonful grated cheese
3 tomatoes
1 egg
1 bread roll
Salt
Pepper
Herbs (parsley, chives, or a pinch or two of dried thyme, basil marjoram, etc.)

NOTE. For this dish it is advisable to use a special tin called a spring-mould. This has a movable bottom, and a spring closure at one side, so that, by releasing the spring, the whole tin can be removed from the finished dish. Old-fashioned tins for making raised pork pies have this device. Another idea would be to use a cake tin, with movable bottom, lined with grease-proof paper. The important thing is to be able to lift out the finished dish without damaging the crust of overlapping potato slices.

Peel and dice the onions and brown them in the butter. Soak the roll, and press out all excess moisture. Work it into the minced meat, together with the skinned and thinly-sliced tomatoes, the onions, and herbs, binding with the beaten egg. Slice the peeled potatoes into slices ⅛ to ¼ inch thick. Grease the mould generously, or, if you are using a paper-lined cake tin, grease the surface of the paper, so that the slices of potato will stay in position until the tin goes into the oven.

Put a layer of potato slices, arranged in overlapping, concentric rings on the bottom of the tin. Line the sides also with overlapping slices, like the scales on a fish. Fill the interior with alternate layers of the meat mixture, and potato slices, seasoning carefully as you go, and ending with a layer of potato slices, arranged in concentric rings, as on the bottom. Sprinkle the grated cheese on top, and bake in a fast oven until the potatoes are crisp and brown. Allow to cool slightly, and then, very carefully, remove the tin. Serve on a hot dish. Tomato sauce (see *Hot Savoury Sauces*) goes very well with this, and so does a green salad.

If you are prepared to take the trouble to prepare this successfully, it is quite an impressive show piece, and one that costs very little.

POTATO SALAD (1)

1 *lb small, firm salad potatoes*
2 *small onions (minced)*
Parsley

Boil the potatoes in their skins. Peel, slice, and while still warm, add the minced onion. Pour over them a dressing made from oil, vinegar, salt, pinch of sugar and lemon juice and let the mixture stand until all the dressing is absorbed. Then mix in a little thick cream, or mayonnaise.

POTATO SALAD (2)

1½ *lbs small, firm salad potatoes*
1 *gill boiling hot, salted water*
1 *small onion*
Salad dressing

Wash the potatoes and boil in their skins. Peel while still hot, and cut into fine slices. Pour over them the boiling, salted water, and leave to stand for five minutes. Lift out the slices carefully with a draining-spoon and lay them in a dish, sprinkling over them the finely-chopped onion. Make a salad dressing, as in the previous Recipe No. 1 and pour over. Allow to stand for at least an hour before serving. A little cream stirred in at the last moment is an improvement. Sprinkle with chopped chives or parsley, if available.

Dumplings and Boiled Puddings

All who are slimming, or cooking for slimmers will, of course, skip this section, but mothers of large hungry families, and those who live in the chillier parts of the country, or who cook for men engaged in heavy manual labour, will find it very useful. Dumplings are particularly popular in mountain districts, but they are considered useful fillers to meals everywhere.

Some cooks prefer to boil them in a large quantity of salted water so that they may move freely, and the lid is left off the pan, so as not to make them soggy. Others prefer to steam them. When they all bob up to the surface it is usually a sign that they are ready and one should be lifted out and opened with two forks. It should be light and dry inside, and light and spongy outside. Lift them out carefully with a draining spoon, and they should be eaten as soon as ready, especially those made with yeast.

A light hand with dumplings is as much prized among German and Austrian cooks, as a light hand with pastry.

The dumpling mixture is formed into small round balls, using well-floured fingers, or, in some cases, two forks, and the wise cook drops one first into the boiling water. If it breaks, the mixture is not stiff enough, and needs more flour, or more breadcrumbs, or more semolina, according to whatever is the basic ingredient. Dumplings will keep their shape better if each is dusted with flour before putting into the boiling water. Some cooks add a teaspoonful of potato flour to the boiling water, in order to help them to keep their shape. Always use a pan deep and wide enough to allow the dumpling to swim.

Finally, do not be discouraged if the first dumpling you try is a failure. Every cook knows that it is the simplest dishes that need the most experience. The English habit of using suet is practically unknown. It would be considered too heavy.

BREAD DUMPLINGS (without egg)

6 stale rolls
About a cupful of milk
1 heaped teaspoonful baking powder
½ lb fine semolina
1–1½ ozs butter or margarine
Salt
A little grated nutmeg

Slice the rolls and soften them in the heated milk, pouring away any excess. Sieve the baking powder thoroughly into the semolina, melt the butter, and well mix all the ingredients, forking them into a thick dough. With a wet spoon cut out round dumpling shapes, and put into boiling, salted water, trying one first. Simmer in uncovered pan for ten minutes.

BREAD DUMPLINGS WITH EGG

6 stale bread rolls
2½ ozs bacon
1 egg
½ pint milk

¼ lb flour
Salt
1–2 teaspoonfuls finely chopped herbs
1 onion

Slice and soften the rolls in the heated milk. Fry the diced bacon and the diced, peeled onion. Press superfluous milk out of the bread and mix into it the salt and the flour. Mix with the bacon and onion in a heavy, enamel saucepan and heat until the mass comes away from the sides. While still hot stir in the beaten egg yolk and then fold in the stiffly-beaten egg whites, and the herbs. Make fairly large dumplings and put into fast boiling salted water. As soon as they are in, lower the heat and simmer for ten to fifteen minutes. Try one, lifting it out carefully with two forks. If not done, give another five minutes, and try again.

HAM DUMPLINGS

4–5 small rolls
¼ lb. smoked ham
2 eggs
1 good gill milk
6–7 oz flour
1 level teaspoonful salt
¼ lb smoked bacon

Dice the bacon and fry. Add the bread, also diced, and stir until it has soaked up all the fat. Whisk the eggs and milk and stir in the flour and salt, which have been well sieved together, and then mix this into the bread and bacon lump. Mince the ham. Using wet hands, form the dough into dumplings, putting a little ham into each. Boil for about fifteen minutes in lightly salted water.

TYROLEAN BACON DUMPLINGS

6 ozs (good measure) stale white bread
6 ozs flour
1 gill milk
2 eggs

¼ lb smoked bacon
Green parsley, or basil leaves

Cut the bacon into small dice and fry lightly. Grater off the crust of the bread. Dice the white crumb and mix with the bacon, leaving to stand for an hour. Whisk up the eggs and milk, the finely chopped parsley or basil, and the flour, and mix with the bread and bacon. Leave to stand for half an hour. Then form into dumplings. Lightly roll these in flour and simmer them in gently boiling water, on a low heat, for about fifteen to twenty minutes. Try one after fifteen minutes.

FLOUR DUMPLINGS

.1½ lbs flour
1 lb cold boiled potatoes
2 eggs
A little milk—or sour milk
Salt
Fried bread croutons

Sieve the flour and salt. Peel and grater the potatoes. Mix with the beaten eggs, and as much milk as is needed to form a smooth, soft dough. This must then be kneaded by hand, until blisters appear. Anyone who has ever kneaded bread dough will know the signs. Fry some diced bread in butter until crisp. Form the dough into dumplings using a wet spoon, and inserting a few croutons of fried bread into the middle of each Simmer gently in salted water, which should be boiling when you put the dumplings in. Try one after fifteen minutes.

SEMOLINA DUMPLINGS

1½ pints milk
12 ozs fine semolina
2–3 eggs
1 level teaspoonful salt
2 heaped tablespoonfuls bread crumbs
1 good ounce butter or margarine
A little butter or margarine for frying the breadcrumbs.

Boil the milk with the butter or margarine and salt, and when it comes to the boil, remove from the heat. Stir in the semolina, a little at a time. Put the pan back on heat and continue to stir until the milk is all soaked up and the mass comes away from the pan. Mix in one beaten egg, and when the semolina has cooled, add the other two eggs, one at a time, beating well. Form into dumplings using wet hands and boil for about ten minutes in slightly salted water. Before serving sprinkle with the fried bread-crumbs.

CHEESE CURD DUMPLINGS

1 *lb cheese curd*
3 *ozs butter or margarine*
2 *eggs*
½ *lb bread crumbs*
1 *level teaspoonful baking powder*
Salt
If like, a little nutmeg, or chopped, green herbs

Pass the curd through a sieve and mix well with the other ingredients—first creaming the eggs and butter together, and beating in the flour a little at a time. The amount used will depend on the wetness of the curd. Form into dumplings with wet hands and boil gently in salted water which should be boiling when they go in. When they come to the surface, they are done.

STEAMED SWEET DUMPLINGS

1 *lb flour*
1 *good oz. yeast*
1 *gill milk*
3 *eggs*
3 *ozs butter*
1 *oz sugar*
Salt

Heat the milk till it is luke-warm, add a pinch of sugar and break the yeast into it. When the yeast has risen to the top, whisk it quickly. Take a $\frac{1}{4}$ lb of the flour, make a hollow in the middle, pour in the beaten milk and yeast, and make a dough and let it rise in a warmed bowl, in a warm place, out of draughts. When it is about twice its original bulk, mix into it the beaten eggs, the sugar, and lastly the butter. Let this dough rise as before. It should be loose enough to flow off the end of a spoon, before the butter is added. Form into small round dumplings and allow them to rise on a floured board, in a warm place, out of draughts. Into a broad-based pan or fire-proof dish, pour milk to a depth of $\frac{3}{4}$ inch and a walnut of butter, a tablespoonful of sugar, and then the little dumplings. Cover the vessel tightly, and, to make sure no steam escapes, put a wet pudding cloth over the lid. Cook for a few minutes on strong heat and then on much reduced heat—about 30 minutes in all. Do not uncover during the whole 30 minutes. When cooked, the dumplings will have soaked up all the milk and will be caramel brown on the under side. Serve with a vanilla-flavoured sauce (See *Sweet Sauces*).

RAW POTATO DUMPLINGS

1–1$\frac{1}{2}$ lbs raw potatoes
8–10 ozs boiled potatoes
About a gill of milk
1 level tablespoonful flour
Salt
Diced, fried bread

Peel the raw potatoes and grater them into a dish with plenty of cold water. Leave to stand, and then thoroughly squeeze out all the liquid, using a jelly-bag, or, better, a potato or fruit press—until a dry mass is left. Peel the boiled potatoes and while still hot, put them through a potato snailer. Mix quickly with the milk and flour and immediately stir in the raw pulp, which has been lightly sprinkled with salt.

With wet hands make large, round dumplings as quickly as you can, stuffing them in the middle with diced, fried bread. Boil in plenty of salted water for about twenty-five minutes. Be careful that the water does not race, or the dumplings will fall apart.

When ready, they should not be hard, but neither should they be slushy and sticky. Cooked by an expert, they can be shaken, and the diced bread will rattle inside—like the pips in a Cox's Orange apple!

BOILED POTATO DUMPLINGS

1½ lbs boiled and peeled potatoes that have gone thoroughly cold
3–4 ozs flour or fine semolina
1–2 eggs
Salt
Diced fried bread

Grater the potatoes, or put them through a snailer. Mix with the beaten eggs, salt, and flour or semolina. The resulting dough must then be well-kneaded until it is firm enough to hold its shape. Using floured hands, form into dumplings, putting into the middle of each a few croutons of fried bread. Boil in salted water for fifteen to twenty minutes. The water should be boiling gently when they go in, and kept boiling gently, not allowed to race. In some country districts, the dumplings are stuffed with minced meat, or fried diced ham, and served with plenty of vegetables, or with sauer-kraut, as a main dish.

YEAST DUMPLINGS

1 lb flour
1 oz yeast
1–2 eggs
1 gill milk
1½ ozs butter or margarine
Salt

Make a yeast dough as follows:— Put the flour in a mixing bowl to warm. Warm the milk to blood-heat, and crumble the yeast into it. Leave to stand for a few minutes until the yeast has risen to the top and then beat yeast and milk briskly together. Make a hollow in the flour and, using the beaten eggs and the yeast mixture, mix into a dough. Knead the dough well, cover lightly with a cloth and stand in a warm place to rise. After about $\frac{3}{4}$–1 hour, knead again and leave to rise again—about half an hour. Roll out on a floured board, and with a glass tumbler, or a pastry cutter, stamp out circular pieces. The dough after rolling should be about one inch thick. Let these rise a little and then boil gently in salted water, in a closely-covered pan. Lift out with a draining-spoon and immediately, using two forks, tear open each dumpling to let the steam escape. Sprinkle with bread crumbs fried in butter. Another method of cooking is to tie a greased cloth over the top of a large saucepan, letting it dip sufficiently over the boiling water so that the dumplings can be laid on it. Instead of a lid, place an up-turned dish of the appropriate size so that it does not touch the dumplings, and steam them. They are done when a knitting needle comes out clean.

These yeast dumplings are very good with roast veal, or they can be eaten as a sweet, with a jam sauce.

Here is a footnote to this section on dumplings. I used to know a German cook, working in an English household, who, when the three little girls came back from a ride on their ponies, would send them out into the garden to select a cherry, or whatever small fruit each fancied. This was then embedded in a very special dumpling and an excited trio hung over the pan, each waiting for hers to pop to the surface. When it did, she was allowed to lift it out on to a warmed plate, where it was thickly sprinkled with cocoa, or, if cook was in a particularly good mood, with grated cooking chocolate, a little dusting of cinnamon, and plenty of brown sugar.

Hot Savoury Sauces

TOMATO SAUCE (1)

2 ozs fat
1½ ozs flour
5–6 tomatoes
3 gills stock
½ teaspoonful grated onion
Salt
Lemon juice
Pinch of sugar
Cream or milk

Blend the flour and the onion into the fat over a gentle heat. Add the sliced tomatoes and fry up together. Add the liquid and other ingredients and boil for fifteen to twenty minutes, stirring continually. Rub through a sieve, add a little cream and re-heat.

$\frac{3}{4}$–1 lb fresh tomatoes
1 oz (generous) butter
1½ ozs flour
1 onion
3 gills stock
1 teaspoonful finely chopped parsley
Salt
Paprika

Cut the tomatoes into small pieces and cook them in a heavy-bottomed pan, without water, over gentle heat until they are soft. Put them through a sieve. Fry the finely chopped onion in fat until soft and sprinkle over them the flour, stirring it in thoroughly. Then add the tomato pulp and the liquid, little by little, beating all the time. When it tastes cooked, season with salt, paprika and parsley, very finely chopped.

BUTTER SAUCE

1 oz (generous) butter
1½ ozs flour
½ teaspoonful grated onion
3 gills stock
2 egg yolks
A little lemon juice
Pinch of sugar
Salt
2 tablespoonfuls milk (cream is better)

Blend the butter into the flour and onion over gentle heat, beat in the stock a bit at a time, add salt, and allow to boil for fifteen minutes, stirring continuously. Mix the egg yolks with the cream or milk and the sugar and lemon juice, beating well together, and stir into the hot sauce, which will thicken. Season to taste. Do not let it boil again but keep hot over a water bath.

CHEESE SAUCE

1 oz butter
1½ ozs flour

½ teaspoonful *grated onion*
.1 gill *water*
½ pint *milk*
1 egg *yolk*
2 ozs finely *grated cheese*
Salt
Cream

Blend butter and onion into the fat over gentle heat until golden brown. Add first the water, stirring continuously, and then the milk. Beat up the egg yolk and cream, and use to thicken the sauce. Season with salt and stir in the cheese. Do not boil again after the cheese is in, but keep hot in a water-bath.

BROWN ONION SAUCE

1½ ozs *fat*
2½ ozs *flour*
3 large *onions*
1 pint *stock*
Salt
A little *vinegar or red wine*

Using a heavy-bottomed pan blend the flour into the fat over strong heat until dark brown, adding the finely chopped onions, bit by bit. When the onions are soft, stir in the stock a little at a time and allow to boil for half an hour. Run through a sieve. Season with salt, and vinegar (or red wine) as preferred.

ONION SAUCE

1½ ozs *butter*
2 ozs *flour*
3 large *onions*
3 gills *water*
Salt
Pepper
Pinch of *sugar*
A little *vinegar*

Slice the peeled onions and fry till golden in the butter. Blend in the flour and then add the water, little by little, stirring continually. Allow to boil until the onions are soft. Season, and pass through a sieve.

SAUCE HOLLANDAISE (1)

1–2 egg yolks
1 tablespoonful water
1 tablespoonful vinegar or lemon juice
1½ ozs butter
Pinch of sugar
Salt
Grated nutmeg

Put all the ingredients except the butter in a double-saucepan (or an enamel dish over boiling water) and beat until just before they come to the boil. Melt the butter, and add it a few drops at a time, beating continually. Beat until the mixture is foamy and keep warm over hot water.

This sauce is delicious on asparagus, cauliflower, broccoli.

SAUCE HOLLANDAISE (2)

1 oz (scanty) flour
1 gill vegetable stock or meat stock
2–3 egg yolks
2 ozs unsalted butter
2–3 tablespoonfuls cream
Pinch of sugar
A little lemon juice or white wine
A pinch of white pepper

Mix the flour to a thin cream with a little of the stock, then stir in the rest of the liquid and boil it, stirring continually until it thickens. Add, alternately, a dab of the butter, which should be very cold and hard, and a little of the beaten egg yolk, beating vigorously all the time. Allow to boil up once and then add the seasoning and lemon juice or wine. Remove at once from the heat and beat up again. Serve at once, or keep hot over boiling water.

This is good on fish, as well as vegetables.

SWEET-SOUR BACON SAUCE

    2 ozs smoked bacon
    1 onion
    1½–2 ozs flour
    3 gills water
    Salt
    Vinegar
    Sugar to taste

Dice the bacon and fry till golden-brown. Add the flour and stir well in and continue frying until the mixture is brown. Then add the diced onions and let them sweat through. Fill up with water and boil, keeping well stirred until it thickens. This sauce is very good on broad beans and peas.

DILL SAUCE

    1½ ozs butter
    1½ ozs flour
    3 gills liquid (half milk and half water)
    2 tablespoonfuls finely chopped dill leaves
    Salt
    A few drops of vinegar
    Pinch of sugar

Blend the flour into the fat over gentle heat until pale gold. Beat in the liquid, little by little and add the vinegar, salt, sugar and bring to the boil. Lastly stir in the chopped dill.

This is served with beef, fish and egg dishes.

MADEIRA SAUCE

    2 ozs butter
    2 ozs flour

3 gills stock
2 tablespoonfuls chopped mushrooms
1 tablespoonful mixed, chopped greens (leek, parsley, chives, celery)
3 tablespoonfuls meat gravy
3 tablespoonfuls madeira wine
Salt

Lightly fry the chopped greens and flour in the melted butter. Stir in the gravy and stock, bring to the boil and strain. Finally add the mushrooms and the wine, after which do not allow to boil again. Season with salt. This is good on tongue, ham, and kidneys.

BROWN BEER SAUCE

1½ ozs butter
1 onion
3 tablespoonfuls chopped greens (leek, celery, parsley, parsnip etc.)
1 level tablespoonful flour
3 gills dark ale
3 ozs gingerbread buttons (or spiced biscuits)
Salt
Lemon juice or vinegar
2 tablespoonfuls black currant jelly (or raspberry juice)

Break up the biscuits and soak till soft in the beer. Chop the onion and vegetables finely and sweat them in the butter. Sprinkle the flour over them and fry until brown. Stir in the beer very slowly a little at a time over gentle heat and then add the softened biscuits. Still stirring bring to the boil and then allow to stand away from the heat for ten minutes. Finally flavour with the lemon juice, salt, and jelly (or raspberry juice).

This sauce is excellent on fresh-water fish, particularly carp.

BÉCHAMEL SAUCE

1½ ozs flour
1½ ozs butter or margarine
1–2 gills milk or meat stock

Lemon juice
Salt
Nutmeg

Blend the flour into the melted butter over gentle heat. Stir in the liquid, little by little and bring to the boil, still stirring. Flavour with salt, lemon juice, and grated nutmeg.

BEATEN EGG SAUCE (Béarnaise)

1 oz butter
1 egg yolk
4 tablespoonfuls water and white wine (two of each)
Salt
Nutmeg
A pinch of sugar
Lemon juice and cream

Divide the butter evenly into three portions. Melt one piece in a small double saucepan (or an enamel dish over boiling water). Beating continuously add a little liquid and half the egg yolk, then another piece of butter, then more liquid, and then the rest of the egg yolk. When the sauce has thickened add the rest of the butter and whisk very hard. Season with salt, a little grated onion and finely chopped chervil and tarragon. Keep the water in the lower pan boiling, but in no circumstances let the sauce boil, or it will run.

COLD SAUCES

These make a wonderful difference to cold meats, cold fish dishes, cold snacks and hors d'oeuvres.

REMOULADE SAUCE

2 hard-boiled eggs
1 finely sliced and peeled gherkin
A little dry mustard

Capers
Onion
Anchovy
A pinch of rubbed herbs (at choice)

All these ingredients are finely chopped (the onion is grated) and well-beaten into the eggs which have also been finely chopped, until a thick, well-blended mayonnaise results. Let this down with thin cream, or top of the milk, to the desired thickness.

This is very good made rather thick and poured over halved, hard-boiled eggs as a variant on egg mayonnaise.

ROQUEFORT SAUCE

These quantities make about 1½ cups of sauce. Very good on cold fish.

½ cup olive oil
½ cup lemon juice
¼ cup crumbled Roquefort
¼ teaspoonful salt
⅛ teaspoonful pepper

Beat all these items well together and store in a screw-top jar or bottle in the refrigerator. Shake well before use, or beat well with a fork if necessary.

GREEN SAUCE

3 hard-boiled egg yolks

Sieve these and mix with olive oil to the consistency of thick cream. Season with salt and pepper. Let down with cream and the juice of not more than half a lemon.

The green colour is obtained by finely chopping chives, celery leaves, half a green leek stem (not the white part), and parsley, and beating well into the sauce. If a darker colour is wanted, add a little spinach.

This is an excellent appetiser with fish.

Sweet Sauces

FRUIT JUICE SAUCE

1 lb of any soft fruit
3 gills water
Sugar
2 level tablespoonfuls cornflour
Lemon juice

Stew the fruit until soft in the water, removing stones if cherries or plums. Sweeten to taste. Make a smooth paste of the cornflour with a little cold water. Stir into the fruit and boil until it thickens, keeping stirred. Put through a sieve and flavour with lemon juice.

FRUIT FOAM SAUCE

3 gills fruit juice
2 egg whites
4 tablespoonfuls caster sugar

Whisk the egg whites into a stiff foam. Fold in the juice and sugar.

APRICOT SAUCE

¼ lb dried apricots
1½ pints water
1½ ozs cornflour
Lemon juice
Pinch of salt
Sugar to taste

Well wash the apricots and soak overnight in 1½ pints water. Next day add a little sugar and bring to the boil. Cook gently until soft. Rub through a sieve, put back into the liquid and thicken by adding the cornflour mixed into a thin cream with a little water, and bring to the boil, stirring all the time.

Flavour with sugar and a little lemon juice.

VANILLA SAUCE

¾ pint milk
1½ ozs sugar
¼ vanilla pod
¾ oz cornflour
1 egg

Boil the milk, sugar and vanilla together and remove from heat for five minutes. Mix the cornflour into a thin cream with a little cold milk. Bring the milk once more to the boil, stirring in the cornflour cream and allow to boil for a short time. Remove the vanilla pod. Continue beating as the mixture cools. When it is cold, stir in the stiffly-beaten egg-white.

Hot Snacks

The purpose of this section is to suggest a few quick dishes that can be served as T.V. suppers, or as lunches for the housewife who eats her mid-day meal alone, or for the girl living in a bed-sitter who grows weary of the eternal egg. All these circumstances exist in Germany, of course, as they do here. It is perhaps easier for the German cook with such a variety of *würste* at her disposal, but, in England these are not cheap, and while a "cold plate" of mixed cold meats and sliced sausage is the easiest, most nourishing and quickest of all snacks, it is by no means the cheapest.

Here, then are a few suggestions.

First, a list. It is often useful to be reminded of familiar dishes when the mind goes completely blank. Recipes for these are not included since they are widely used in England.

Egg mayonnaise. Try it with Remoulade sauce instead of mayonnaise.

Stuffed hard-boiled eggs.

Hard-boiled eggs sliced, sprinkled with grated cheese, a little egg—milk—flour batter poured over them and baked for 15–20 minutes.

Poached eggs on toast served with one of the piquant sauces, i.e. anchovy, mustard or tomato.

Fried eggs. Try breaking them over lightly-fried bacon slices.

Scrambled eggs with grated cheese.

Scrambled eggs with fried tomato slices.

Omelettes with various fillings, i.e. chopped, cooked mushrooms, finely chopped ham, meat or veal stew, young peas, chopped cooked asparagus, finely-sliced cheese, chopped green herbs, minced cold chicken in a white sauce.

Slimmers will prefer open sandwiches—one slice brown or rye-bread only.

Sausages grilled or fried. Try serving them with apple purée, or apple and horseradish sauce or tomatoes fried with onions.

Tomatoes stuffed with scrambled egg and onion (grated), and baked in a hot oven for 5–10 minutes.

Tomatoes stuffed with shrimps in Remoulade sauce.

Tomatoes stuffed with Italian salad.

STUFFED APPLES

Cut half inch thick bread rounds and spread with butter. Cut small cooking apples in halves and remove the core. Place one half on each bread round, cut side uppermost. Sprinkle the cut surface with lemon juice. Fill the core hole and spread the cut surface with any soft, processed cheese. Cut little matchlike strips of smoked bacon or ham, and lay them in a wheel-spoke design on the top of the cheese.

Bake in a hot oven about 15 minutes and serve immediately.

CHEESE SLICES

8 thick slices of white bread
1–2 eggs
3 gills milk
4 ozs flour
Sliced packet cheese
Butter or margarine
Salt

Soften the bread slices in half the milk. Lay them on a well-greased tin or fire-proof dish. Beat up the egg in the rest of the milk. Stir in the flour—add salt—a little kümmel (or a pinch of carraway seeds) and the finely grated cheese. Pile the resulting creamy mixture on the buttered bread slices and bake in a hot oven for 30 minutes. Cut into fingers and serve with green salad.

EGG ON CHEESE SLICES

4 eggs
4 slices of toasted white bread
4 slices of processed cheese
2 tablespoonfuls grated cheese

Butter the slices thinly and lay a slice of cheese on each. Soft boil the eggs, and shelling each carefully, place one on each slice. Sprinkle thickly with grated cheese and bake in a very hot oven until the cheese runs and begins to brown.

CHEESE TOAST

4 thick slices of white toasting bread
3½ ozs grated cheese (Cheshire is good, or Lancashire, or any cheese that crumbles and melts easily)
2½ ozs butter
Salt
Paprika
Chopped parsley, or chives

Cream the butter and mix in the crumbled cheese. Flavour with salt, paprika and stir in the chopped parsley or chives. Make a pyramid of the resulting mixture on each bread slice, and grill, having first heated the grill so that it is fierce.

HAM CHEESE SLICES

4 thick slices of white bread
Butter
Mustard
4 slices of raw (or cooked) smoked ham
4 slices of Swiss cheese (Gruyère or Emmenthaler)
Paprika

Spread the bread with butter, and, very thinly with mustard. Lay on each one slice of ham and one slice of cheese. Heat up the grill until it is fierce and grill the slices for about 3 minutes.

MEAT OR SAUSAGE SLICES

4 thick slices of minced ham—or pork meat, or one of the soft wurst
4 slices of white bread
4 slices of Swiss cheese
Milk or cider
Fat for frying

Soak the bread slices in the milk (or cider) and lay on each a slice of the meat cut to the same size. Then top off each with a slightly smaller slice of cheese. Heat the fat in a frying-pan and lay the slices in it. Cover, and fry on very fast heat until the cheese melts and the whole is crisp. Serve at once.

EGGS WITH YOUNG PEAS

½ lb young shelled peas
2 eggs
½ cup meat stock
1 oz butter or margarine
Salt
Grated onion
Green herbs

Simmer the peas very gently in hot butter or margarine for 15 minutes on a low heat. Beat up the eggs in the stock with the finely-grated onion and salt and pour over the peas. Shake the pan gently and leave on the side, or on a very low heat, until the egg mixture sets. Sprinkle with chopped parsley or chives and serve with fried or sauté potatoes.

EGG AND POTATO BAKE

1½ lbs cold boiled potatoes
3 eggs
1 lb tomatoes
1 tablespoonful finely grated onion
2 tablespoonfuls chopped parsley
3 gills sour milk or yoghourt (fresh milk can be used if preferred)
Butter
Fat for frying

Peel the potatoes and slice them. Slice the tomatoes. Fry the onion and parsley in a little fat until the onions are translucent. Well grease a dish and lay the potatoes, tomatoes and the onion mixture in layers. Beat up the eggs with the milk (or sour milk, or yoghourt) and add a little salt. Pour over the contents of the dish. Spread little dabs of butter all over the top surface and bake in a moderate to hot oven for about an hour—or until the potatoes and tomatoes appear to be cooked.

MIXED SAVOURY TOAST

6 slices of white bread
¼ lb diced ham (raw or cooked)
3 hard-boiled eggs
3 tomatoes
Mustard
Paprika
Grated cheese

A little butter
Chopped chives

Butter the bread and spread thinly with mustard. Sprinkle with chives, then a layer of diced ham, then a layer of sliced hard-boiled egg, then a layer of tomato slices. Sprinkle thickly with grated cheese (Parmesan is good) and grill for about three minutes under a very fierce grill.

LIVER SLICES

4 thick slices of white bread
$\frac{1}{4}$ lb liver
2 ozs gammon
1 small onion
1 egg
1 heaped tablespoonful flour
Salt
Pepper
Parsley

Butter the bread slices. Skin the liver and put it, and the onion and gammon, and parsley through the mincer. Stir the egg and flour together as for a batter and mix this into the mince. Season with salt and pepper. Spread thickly on the bread slices and grill under maximum heat for about three minutes.

SCRAMBLED EGGS WITH WURST

4 eggs
4 tablespoonfuls milk
Slices of mettwurst, or mortadella, or any of the soft, cooked
    sausages
Fat for frying

Beat up the egg, milk and salt. Melt the fat and lightly fry the sausage slices. Pour the egg mixture over them and allow to set over gentle heat. Fried potatoes and a sharp, lettuce salad are the best accompaniments.

2 *slices per person of mortadella, or any similar soft wurst. Be sure that the outer skin is intact.*

Fry the slices very quickly in very hot fat so that the rings of outer skin contract, pulling the slices into little ound, shallow baskets. Fill these, with any mixture of chopped cooked vegetables, scrambled eggs, savoury rice, cheese and bacon diced, rice with apple sauce, etc., that you may fancy. They can be served sitting on a slice of buttered toast, or on a little mound of mashed potato, or on boiled noodles or boiled rice.

PORK SAUSAGES IN BEER

1 *lb pork sausages*
1 *onion*
½ *pint brown ale*
Flour
Salt
Pepper
Fat for frying

Steep the sausages for a few minutes in boiling water, which extracts surplus fat. Dry them, roll them in flour and brown them in hot fat in a heavy frying pan. Cut the onion into rings and add it with the beer, to the sausages. Cover the pan, and braise gently until the onion rings are soft. Make a flour thickening with a little cold water or milk and stir into the gravy to thicken it. Season with salt and pepper.

PORK SAUSAGES IN SWEET–SOUR SAUCE

1 *lb sausages*
1 *onion*
Flour
Water
Sugar
Vinegar
Fat for frying
Pepper
Salt

Fry the sausages until well browned all over in hot fat, and lift out on to a warmed dish. Chop the onion finely and brown in the sausage gravy. Sprinkle freely with flour and add as much water as you need for sauce, according to the number of servings. Then add salt, pepper, vinegar and sugar until you have the desired sweet-sour flavour. Then put the sausages in the liquid and, keeping it hot, but not allowing it to boil, let them stand in it for ten minutes.

HAM WITH CHICORY

Wash and well dry the chicory, keeping it whole. Lay side by side on the bottom of a pan large enough to take as many pieces as you need in a single layer. Pour over them enough milk to cover the bottom of the pan and a substantial knob of butter. Cover the pan and braise on a very low light and an asbestos mat (to prevent sticking). When the chicory is tender, season lightly with salt. Lift out and wrap a slice of cooked ham round each piece of chicory and lay carefully side by side in a pie dish. Place in a hot oven for five minutes to heat the ham. Make a white sauce by adding flour, and a little lemon juice to the juice in the braising pan, and pour over just before serving.

Cold Snacks

COLD PLATE

Arrange on each plate slices of all your favourite würst and salami, little mounds of cold, peeled shrimps sitting on thick slices of raw tomato, a little smoked salmon (or a lot if you can afford it!) one or two slices of raw, garlic-cured ham (the Italian prosciutto). Use your imagination and add any other cold meat or savoury liked by your family. In the middle of the plate a slice of one of the tougher cheeses (Emmenthaler, Gouda, Edam) folded into a cone and filled with cream cheese.

Garnish with sprigs of parsley and sliced, pickled gherkins, or chives and cocktail onions. Serve plenty of rye (or wholemeal) bread and generous pats of butter.

CHEESE PLATE

Arrange on each plate slices of Emmenthaler, Edam, Cheshire,

Gruyère, Roquefort or Gorgonzola—one or two of the small, packet blended cheeses (cheese with ham, cheese with celery, cheese with onion etc.), and any other type of cheese you fancy. Add cheese straws and pretzels and round the edge of the plate, radishes cut into fancy shapes, parsley, salted almonds or peanuts. Serve on a side plate a generous pat of butter and two or three slices per person of rye bread. If German bread is disliked by the family, wholemeal may be substituted. Have available horseradish cream, mayonnaise and mustard for those who like to add a bite to their cheese. A few capers and cocktail onions scattered about the plate help to add bite.

COLD MEAT PLATE

This comes more expensive, but is very good. Use cold meats, cold chicken or turkey, smoked salmon and slices of cheese and pad out with slices of salami and wurst.

LIPTAUER CHEESE

$\frac{1}{2}$ lb cheese curd
2 ozs butter or 1 gill of sour cream
4 ozs grated Emmenthaler (or Gruyère) cheese
1 small grated onion
A little mustard powder
A little paprika powder

Beat all these ingredients together with a fork until creamy. Some people add an egg yolk.

Lay a lettuce leaf on a slice of buttered rye (or wholemeal) bread. If you like Pumpernickel or Vollkornbrot, use a slice of either. Form the Liptauer into little balls about the size of a walnut. Dust each with paprika and lay on the lettuce leaf, using cheese straws or pieces of pretzel to separate the cheese balls.

Salads

These are as varied as the salads of any other European country. The German cook is fond of using all kinds of cold, cooked vegetables—cauliflower, peas, French beans, carrots, cooked celery, button mushrooms and asparagus. She will have cooked all these in meat stock to add flavour and, when cold, she will arrange them, according to colour, in radiating lines like the spokes of a wheel, sprinkling generously with chopped parsley or chives, and garnishing with slices of raw tomato, gherkins, anchovy fillets, capers, etc.

In all cold salads, slices of hard-boiled egg are used freely. Home-made mayonnaise is better as being more delicately flavoured than the commercial varieties.

SMOKED-TONGUE SALAD

½ lb sliced, smoked ox tongue
6 oz cold boiled potatoes and cold cooked celery mixed.

3 small tomatoes
1 onion
Meat stock
Mayonnaise

Dice the tongue, potatoes and celery. Grate the onion, cut the tomatoes into small pieces and put all ingredients into the meat stock, using just enough to be soaked up. Pour away any excess liquid after the mixture has stood for half an hour. Stir in a little mayonnaise.

ASPARAGUS SALAD (Quick)

1 carton quick-frozen short asparagus
½ carton quick-frozen young peas
1 oz diced, cooked ham
Tomato
Parsley

Thaw and drain peas and asparagus. Cut each asparagus piece lengthways once, and slice tomatoes finely. After tossing asparagus, peas, ham, and tomato slices in a paprika dressing, line the salad bowl with tender, inner leaves of round lettuce and arrange the mixture on them.

For the Paprika dressing:
4 tablespoonfuls olive oil
2 tablespoonfuls lemon juice
Salt, sugar, and a few shakes of powdered paprika

CHICORY SALAD

3–4 clubs of chicory
4 hard-boiled eggs.
Fresh lemon juice
1 Red pepper

Well soak the chicory with plenty of lemon juice. Halve the eggs, remove the yolks and cut the whites into fine strips. Remove the core from the pepper and cut the flesh into fine strips. Cut the chicory into rings. Arrange all the strips and rings on lettuce leaves in a salad bowl and pour over them a dressing, made as follows:—Work the four egg yolks and about three to four tablespoons of olive oil into a thick cream. Then stir in two tablespoons of vinegar, little by little, and add mustard, sugar and salt to taste.

WHITE CABBAGE SALAD WITH ALMONDS

2 oz blanched and chopped almonds
1 lb raw, shredded white cabbage
3 tablespoonfuls melted butter or margarine
3 gills milk
2 tablespoonfuls flour
1 teaspoonful curry powder
Salt

Fry the chopped almonds lightly in the butter. Heat the milk, add salt and the shredded cabbage and let it come to the boil once. Drain off the milk into another saucepan and stir into it the flour and curry powder. With the aid of a knob of butter, this can be stirred into a thickish sauce. Let it cook for a minute or two, stirring all the time—five minutes should suffice. Pour it over the cabbage, sprinkle the fried nuts on top and serve at once.

ASPARAGUS SALAD WITH CUCUMBER

1 lettuce
1 small cucumber
3 tomatoes
1 lb asparagus
1 gill thin cream
Small bottle cocktail olives
Vinegar
Salt
Pepper
Sugar
Oil

Slice the cucumber very thinly, leaving on most of the outer skin. Cut the tomatoes into eighths. Well-drain the cooked asparagus and mix all the ingredients together with the chopped olives. Make a dressing from a little of the asparagus water, cream, vinegar, mustard, salt, pepper, sugar and oil, as for a French dressing and toss the salad in it. Serve with curried rice.

ORANGE AND ASPARAGUS SALAD

This is a good way of using up cold chicken leftovers.

    ½ lb cold chicken scraps
    4 oranges
    ½ lb cooked asparagus
    2 tablespoonfuls cream
    4 tablespoonfuls mayonnaise
    1 large cooking apple
    Lemon juice

Dice the chicken, and the peeled and cored apple, and leave to stand, well-sprinkled with fresh lemon juice, while you prepare the rest of the salad. Cut the asparagus into half-inch pieces and mix with the flesh from the oranges (kitchen scissors are the quickest way of dealing with the orange flesh). Beat the cream and mayonnaise well together and stir all the ingredients into it. This salad should be served well chilled.

COLD PORK SALAD

    ½ lb sliced, cold, roast pork
    ½ lb cold, boiled potatoes
    2 apples
    1 onion
    2 small pickled gherkins
    6 anchovy fillets
    Mayonnaise

Dice the meat, the peeled potatoes, the peeled raw apples and finely chop the gherkins. Grate the onion and chop finely the anchovy fillets. Mix the whole into the mayonnaise.

3 *salted herrings*
1 *lb cold boiled potatoes*
2 *cooking apples*
1 *pickled gherkin*
1 *teaspoonful mixed herbs*

The herrings should be well soaked in cold water for twenty-four hours. Skin them and remove the flesh from the bones. Cut into small pieces. Skin the potatoes and dice them. Peel and core the apples and dice them, and the gherkin and put all these ingredients into a shallow dish. Make an oil and vinegar dressing with mustard flavouring and beat it with a fork until it thickens. Stir in the finely-grated onion and the herbs. Pour over the contents of the dish and stir all together. This salad improves the longer it is left to stand before serving.

COLD FISH AND ORANGE SALAD

$\frac{1}{2}$ *lb cooked cold fish*
2 *medium-sized oranges*
1 *pickled gherkin*

Remove any skin and bones from the fish. Peel the oranges and remove white pith and any pips. Cut up into small pieces using kitchen scissors. Break the fish into small pieces, and chop the gherkin. Stir all these ingredients into mayonnaise and serve in the centre of a ring of cold, boiled rice.

COLD BEEF AND ORANGE SALAD

$\frac{1}{2}$ *lb cold beef cut into dice*
2 *oranges*
The juice of a third orange
$2\frac{1}{2}$ *oz rice*
Salt
Sugar
Lemon juice
Curry powder
Mayonnaise

Boil the rice in salted water. Drain well and allow to cool. Add water to the orange juice until there is 1 gill of liquid. Stir in cornflour sufficient to thicken, bringing to the boil as you stir. While it is still hot, beat in two or three tablespoons home-made mayonnaise. Flavour with salt, sugar, lemon juice and a very little curry powder. There should only be a very delicate flavour of curry. Stir in the diced beef, the rice, and the oranges, also cut into small pieces.

ASPIC JELLY

This is very popular in the preparation of cold snacks and hors d'oeuvres. A good, strongly flavoured meat, fish or vegetable stock, according to what is to be jellied, is the basis. Vinegar is added, in the proportion of 1 gill to every $1\frac{1}{2}$ pints stock. This is boiled up with a bay leaf, a few peppercorns and a little grated onion. The gelatine is softened in cold water, well-drained and melted in the hot liquid. Follow the directions on the packet for quantities of gelatine. Once the gelatine is in, do not boil again. Pour over the meat, fish or vegetables to be jellied, and stand in a very cold place to set. Unless you have made an extra stiff mixture, let it stand over night. To turn out for serving, dip the container for a second or two in boiling water. With the aid of aspic, very elaborate colour designs can be achieved by arranging different coloured vegetables in a small, individual glass dish, and pouring over them enough aspic to cover. This, when set, will hold the design in position. One of the most popular, and easiest is to arrange asparagus sticks, or whole French beans, or long strips of carrot, like the spokes of a wheel, using half a tomato, or half a hard-boiled egg as the hub. Once these are safely set in just enough aspic to anchor, but not cover them, the spaces between can be filled in with all kinds of chopped, cooked vegetables and any other savoury 'bits' available, and the whole set by the addition of more aspic. Using a little imagination it is very easy to achieve some spectacular effects.

Pancakes

Basic pancake batter is of two kinds. For thin pancakes, such as are rolled round a filling, the whole eggs are beaten into the milk. For thicker pancakes the yolks and whites are separated, and the stiffly-beaten whites folded in just before cooking. *Schmarrn* a stiffer batter that can be cut into strips when cooked is made by using more flour. *Schmarrn* batter, in which the eggs have been separated, makes a very airy-looking concoction, when baked in a fast oven, or dropped in small bits into boiling fat.

All pancake batter is much improved by being left to stand several hours, and well-beaten again before using. No baking powder is needed to make it rise. The secret lies in the amount of beating, which beats air into the mixture, and in always putting your batter into a hot, well-greased container—a hot frying-pan for pancakes, a hot tin, well lined with hot fat, and a very hot oven for batter puddings. For sweetening batter always use fine, caster sugar.

½ lb flour
3 gills milk and water (half and half)
2–3 eggs (according to size)
Salt

Sieve together the flour and salt into a mixing bowl. Make a hollow in the middle and pour into it the egg yolks well beaten with a little milk. Stir the flour into it, and, adding the milk and water a little at a time, keep on beating, using an open, wire whisk, until all the liquid is in. The batter should be of a consistency that runs slowly off the spoon. Leave to stand for half an hour—longer if possible. Then fold in the stiffly-beaten egg whites.

A heavy frying-pan is best. Use a little fat that is very hot, but not smoking and use a good spoonful of the mixture for each pancake, letting it run thinly over the bottom of the pan. Cook very quickly, golden-brown on both sides.

Two favourite ways of serving pancakes is to pile them one on top of another, like a layer cake, spreading each one with heated marmalade, and the top one with icing sugar, or grated chocolate and a sprinkle of sugar, instead of the marmalade.

EMPEROR'S PANCAKE (Kaiserschmarrn)

¼ lb. flour
1 level tablespoonful caster sugar
8 tablespoonfuls milk
1 oz raisins or sultanas
Cinnamon
Sugar
Fat for frying

Sieve the flour, sugar and salt into the mixing bowl. Make a hollow in the middle and beat in the two egg yolks, one at a time, and then the milk, a tablespoonful at a time, until you have a batter dough. Leave to stand for as long as you can spare the time, but for at least half an hour, and then fold in the stiffly-beaten egg whites. Pour into a hot, greased, heavy frying-pan to a depth of about ¼ inch. Sprinkle the raisins or sultanas on top, and carefully turn over as soon as the underside is golden. Using two forks, divide the pancake into small strips, fry a minute or two longer. Sprinkle with powdered sugar, and a dusting of cinnamon. Some cooks prefer to use currants, and some sprinkle a few ground almonds before turning the pancake.

As the whole is cooked very quickly, the dried fruit should be well-soaked in boiling water to soften it before using.

PALATSCHINKEN

>   7 oz flour
>   1 gill milk
>   3 eggs
>   Fat for frying

Filling:

>   3 eggs
>   ½ lb curd cheese
>   3½ oz butter
>   5–6 oz sugar (caster)
>   Salt
>   Grated lemon rind

Sieve the flour and salt into the mixing bowl. Make a hollow in the middle. Pour into it the three eggs beaten into the milk and, working outwards, gradually beat in all the flour. Leave this batter mixture to stand while you prepare the filling.

Cream the butter and sugar as for a sponge and then beat into it three egg yolks, the lemon rind, and the curd which has been rubbed through a sieve. Finally, fold in the stiffly-beaten egg whites.

Fry a large thin pancake in a hot, greased, heavy frying-pan. When golden on both sides, lift out onto a heated dish, spread with the curd filling, roll up quickly and sprinkle freely with powdered sugar.

An alternative method is to make several smaller pancakes, spread and roll up as above, and place in a well-buttered tin, in a hot oven for ten minutes.

APPLE BATTER (Appleschmarrn)

2 apples
1 egg
2 egg whites
2½–3 oz flour
Milk
Sugar
Ground cinnamon
Salt
Fat for frying

Make a pancake batter from flour, salt, whole egg, and as much milk as is needed to get the consistency you want. When this has been well beaten, fold in the stiffly-beaten egg whites. Pour into a hot, well-buttered heavy frying-pan, enough of the batter to cover the bottom to a depth of about ¼ inch. As soon as one side is golden-brown, spread the top with very thin apple slices, so that they sink into the soft, uncooked batter. Sprinkle with dried breadcrumbs and either toss or turn over. When golden-brown, divide into small pieces with two forks, and fry a little longer, shaking the pan gently to prevent sticking.

Serve with a generous sprinkling of powdered sugar, and a dusting of ground cinnamon.

Some cooks partly cook the apples first by frying the very thin slices in a little butter and allowing to cool before putting in the batter.

APPLE FRITTERS (with a difference!)

1½ oz butter
2½ oz sugar
2 egg yolks
¼ lb flour
1 oz ground nuts
2 stiffly-beaten egg whites
2 tablespoonfuls rum
3 large apples—peeled, cored and cut in rings

Sieve the flour and the ground nuts together. Cream the butter and sugar, beat in the egg yolks and then, little by little, beating strongly, the flour and nuts. Lastly fold in the egg whites which have been beaten until very stiff. Flour both sides of the apple rings, dip them in the batter and fry until golden brown in hot deep fat, preferably one of the vegetable fats. Lift out, drain, and sprinkle with icing sugar. Some cooks beat the rum in with the egg yolks. Some prefer it poured over the cooked fritter, before dusting with sugar.

SALZBURGER NOCKERL

Although this is named after the Austrian city where it originated, it has been borrowed by Germany. It is one of the most famous of the dishes based on a butter and egg batter.

> 1½ oz butter
> 3 oz caster sugar
> 5–6 eggs (separated)
> 2 tablespoonfuls flour

For cooking it:

> 4 tablespoonfuls milk or cream
> 1½ oz butter
> Vanilla sugar to flavour

Make a batter by creaming the sugar into the butter and gradually beating the egg yolks. Then beat in the flour, a little at a time, and lastly, stir in the stiffly-beaten egg whites.

Heat the milk (or cream) and the second 1½ oz butter in a fire-proof dish. Lay the batter mass carefully in it and allow to rise in a fast oven for 10 minutes.

Dust freely with vanilla-flavoured sugar just before serving.

Another method of cooking the Nockerl

Have ready a heavy frying-pan with hot, melted butter, and pour in the batter as for an omelette. Cook over a gentle heat until the underside is golden. Cut quickly into pieces with a very sharp knife and turn each piece upside down to firm the top surface. Do not let the pieces brown, but lift them out carefully using a fish-slice or draining-spoon. Sprinkle thickly with icing sugar and serve at once.

EGG MERINGUE BATTER

If successful this looks so spectacular that it is a wonderful show piece for a young hostess—or indeed for any hostess.

3 eggs (separated)
1 level tablespoonful flour
1 level tablespoonful milk
Salt
1 oz caster sugar
1½ oz butter for cooking

Beat the egg whites very stiffly. Beat the egg yolks, milk and salt thoroughly and fold into the egg whites. Also fold in very lightly the well-sieved flour. Pour the mixture to a depth of about ¾ inch in two flame-proof dishes which have been well buttered and fry until the undersides are brown. Then put both dishes into a moderate oven to rise for about 10 minutes. Lift out one piece carefully onto a warmed dish and spread with a sweet filling (jam or marmalade). Lay the other piece on it, sandwich fashion and serve at once.

Shapes and Creams

SEMOLINA SHAPE

¼ lb sugar
1 oz (generous) butter
5 oz semolina
Vanilla to taste

Bring milk, butter and sugar to the boil, keeping stirred. Stir
the semolina gradually into the hot milk. Keep on stirring until
all the milk is soaked up. Rinse the mould in very cold water
and while still wet, put the mixture into it. Stand in a cool place
until set. Serve with a sweet sauce.

CHOCOLATE SHAPE

1½ oz cocoa (or 2 oz finely grated chocolate)
2 oz cornflour
3 gills milk

3½ oz sugar
Pinch of salt

Mix cornflour and cocoa with a few tablespoons of cold milk into
a thin paste. Boil the rest of the milk with a very little water, the
salt and the sugar. Then stir in the cold creamed cocoa and cornflour. Let the mixture boil for three minutes, stirring continuously.
Pour into a mould that has been rinsed in very cold water, and
stand in a cool place to set.

RICE SHAPE

3 gills milk
5 oz rice
3 oz sugar
½ oz white gelatine
½ vanilla pod
Pinch of salt

Wash the rice thoroughly and boil it with the salt, sugar and
vanilla pod in milk until it swells. Take out the vanilla pod, and
stir in the gelatine, which has been softened in cold water. When
the mixture has cooled, stir in 2 tablespoons maraschino and a
gill of thick cream. Put the whole into a well-buttered ring shape.
Put in a very cool place. Turn out onto the serving dish and fill
the centre with cooked cherries, or apricot halves, or peach
quarters, cooked in a sweet syrup, and, by way of decoration,
arrange a ring of whatever fruit is chosen, round the base of the
rice.

If preferred leave out the maraschino, substituting a fruit syrup.

SEMOLINA AND ALMOND SHAPE

1½ pints milk
6 oz sugar
6–7 oz semolina
1½ oz raisins or sultanas
2 eggs
Pinch of salt

Grated rind of half a lemon

3–4 tablespoonfuls ground almonds

Boil the milk with sugar and salt. Stir in the semolina a little at a time, until it thickens. Add the grated lemon rind and the well-washed raisins. Stir the egg yolks into 2 tablespoons of the hot mixture. Remove from the heat and stir this egg mixture into the rest. Lastly, stir in the ground almonds and the stiffly-beaten egg whites. Put the mixture into a wet mould that has been rinsed in very cold water.

Stand to set in a very cool place.

VANILLA CREAM

1½ pints milk

Pinch of salt

2–3 eggs (according to size)

Small piece of vanilla pod

2½–3½ oz sugar (according to number of eggs)

1½–2 oz cornflour (according to number of eggs)

2–3 tablespoonfuls cream

Bring the milk, salt and vanilla to the boil. Make the egg yolks, sugar and cornflour into a smooth cream with a little cold milk. Stir this into the hot mixture, on low heat, and let it boil right up the pan. Remove from heat, and while still hot, fold in the stiffly-beaten egg whites. Lastly, as the mixture cools, whip the cream, and fold it in.

HAZELNUT CREAM

2 oz hazel nuts

2–3 egg yolks

1½ oz sugar

1 gill milk

1 teaspoonful cornflour

½ gill thick cream

Vanilla flavouring

½ oz gelatine

Roast the nuts in the oven or in a frying-pan until the brown skin can be rubbed off between two pieces of cloth (or with the fingers). Grind them in a nut mill.

Soften the gelatine in a little hot water. Beat well together the milk, cornflour and egg yolks. Add the sugar and vanilla flavouring and over a low heat, stirring continually, let it boil up the pan once. Remove from the heat, stir in the gelatine, and continue stirring until the mixture begins to cool. Fold in the stiffly-beaten egg whites. Whip the cream and mix the ground nuts into it. Fold this into the mixture. Put into a greased mould and put into the refrigerator. After turning out of the mould, decorate with whole nuts, glacé cherries, and little rosettes of whipped cream.

LEMON CREAM

(This is very good for tempting invalids who have lost their desire for food.)

> 3 gills milk
> 3–4 egg yolks
> 2½–3½ oz sugar
> ½–1 oz white gelatine
> 3–4 egg whites
> ½–1 gill whipped cream
> Grated ring of 2 lemons
> Juice of 1 lemon

Boil the milk. Mix together the egg yolks, sugar and grated lemon peel and stir into the hot milk over gentle heat and keep stirring until the mixture rises up the pan once. Remove from heat and go on beating for a minute or so. Soften the gelatine in hot water and beat it into the hot mixture. Stir in the lemon juice. As the mixture begins to stiffen, stir in the cream. Beat in one third of the stiffly-beaten egg whites and gently fold in the rest. Pour into a glass dish, and stand in a cool place.

Fruit Compotes

These are so popular in Germany that they must be mentioned
here, even though the British housewife knows all about stewing
fruit. Every conceivable variety of fruit is made into compotes.
If the meal has been heavy, or rich, they provide the final course,
served alone, in small individual glass dishes, without cream. If,
on the other hand, the hostess does not consider that her guests
have been adequately filled up, she will serve one of the sweet
dumplings, or boiled puddings, with a little jug of hot fruit
compote beside each plate, to serve as a sauce.

Lemon juice, grated lemon rind, and frequently a little cinnamon,
is added to the water and boiled up before the fruit is added, to
simmer gently until soft. Do not overcook.

For soft fruit the minimum of water is used, so as not to dilute the
natural juice. Dried fruit (apple rings, plums, apricots, peaches
etc.) is soaked over night, and the water in which it has soaked is

boiled up with the lemon or cinnamon flavouring before the fruit is added.

The sourer fruits, gooseberries, rhubarb, made into a compote, are sometimes served with the richer, greasier meat or bacon dishes, as we serve apple sauce with pork. To save sugar, a German cook will cut the rhubarb into pieces of the desired length and steep them in boiling water, before beginning to stew them. Sugar should not be added to any fruit until five minutes before it is cooked.

If desired the cooked fruit can be taken out of the juice, put through a sieve, and after whipped cream and/or stiff egg whites have been stirred into it, served as fruit fool:

The remaining juice, slightly thickened with cornflour and served hot, becomes a sauce for the various dumpling, batter, or boiled pudding shapes, or, served cold, a sauce for ice-cream dishes.

Here are two fruit novelties.

ICED GRAPES

Wash and carefully dry a bunch of green grapes and put them in the refrigerator. When they are well chilled, sprinkle very thickly with icing sugar and put back into the refrigerator until wanted. They will appear to be covered with snow.

BANANA BOATS

Small canary bananas
Juice of a lemon
Whipped cream
Sugar
Ground almonds
1 tablespoonful rum
Various small, round fruits, as available (fresh cherries, grapes, raspberries, etc.)

Slit the bananas long ways and carefully remove the flesh leaving two boat-shaped empty, half-skins. Crush the banana flesh with a fork and mix into it, sugar, cream, almonds and rum. Put this mixture back into the skins, dot the other whole fruits here and there, sprinkle generously with icing sugar, and decorate with piped, whipped cream.

Finally—have you tried hot chocolate sauce on cold stewed fruits? It is particularly good on large halved pears, or peaches, which can be either raw, stewed, or tinned. However, if you use tinned fruit, strain away every trace of the sweet syrup, and rinse the portions lightly in cold water.

Sponges

Every cook knows that the secret of a successful sponge lies in the beating. There are still a few die-hards (I am one of them) who believe that beating with an open wire whisk, is still the best method for it lifts more air into the mixture than is possible with any of the mechanical mixers. On the other hand, mechanical mixers are splendid for making egg whites really stiff.

Here is the sponge mixture for a variety of cakes.

$\frac{1}{2}$ *lb flour*
4 *oz butter or margarine*
4 *oz sugar*
1 *heaped teaspoonful baking powder*
2 *eggs*
4 *tablespoonfuls milk*
Vanilla flavouring (optional)
Grated lemon peel (optional)

Cream the butter until fluffy, then beat in the sugar and eggs, a little of each alternately. Continue beating until the mixture is pale in colour and really light and fluffy.

Sieve together the flour, salt and baking powder several times and then stir, a little at a time, into the creamed mixture, adding vanilla flavouring and lemon rind as you go. Add milk until you have a smooth, soft cream that will run off the end of the mixing spoon. Have in readiness a well-greased tin, lined with grease-proof paper. Some cooks grease both sides of the paper and scatter finely ground dried bread crumbs before putting the mixture into the tin. Bake in a pre-heated medium oven. Do not open the oven door for at least 20 minutes. Then test carefully with a fine knitting needle.

This is also the mixture for a variety of sponge cakes. Most commonly seen is the Napfkuchen, which looks like an up-turned pudding with a hole in the middle. German cooks make constant use of a fluted baking tin in the form of a ring. The resulting cake, with a hole through its middle is easier to cut than ours, and cooks more quickly and evenly. In the case of marble cake, the various coloured doughs can be dropped into the ring tin in a large number of very small quantities, giving an elaborate design when cut.

NAPFKUCHEN WITH CREAM CHEESE

4 oz butter or margarine
2 eggs
5 oz sugar
½ lb fresh cream cheese curd
12 oz flour
Grated rind of half a lemon
Vanilla flavouring
3 oz each of ground almonds and sultanas
2 teaspoonfuls baking-powder

Cream the butter. Put the curd through a sieve, and cream it into the butter, adding sugar, egg yolks, lemon and vanilla. Sieve together the flour and baking-powder, and beat this in a little at a time. Roll the sultanas in flour and stir them into the mixture with the ground almonds. Finally fold in the stiffly-beaten egg whites. The mixture should be fairly stiff. Add a little milk only if necessary.

Put into a fluted ring tin that has been well buttered and bake in a moderate oven for slightly over the hour.

When turned out sprinkle with icing sugar, or ice with a thin water icing.

MARBLE CAKE

7 oz butter
$\frac{1}{2}$ lb sugar
3–4 eggs
1 lb flour
$\frac{1}{2}$ gill milk
2 heaped teaspoonfuls baking-powder
Bitter almond flavouring, or a few ground, bitter almonds

For the chocolate sponge:

$\frac{3}{4}$–1 oz cocoa
2 oz sugar
1 tablespoonful rum
Milk if needed

Cream together butter, sugar and eggs. Sieve together flour and baking-powder and beat into the butter cream little by little. Finally add the flavouring, the rum, and the milk.

Take away one third of the mixture, and to this third add the cocoa powder which has been passed through a sieve with the 2 oz of sugar.

Have in readiness a well-buttered ring tin. Put the white mixture in first, and then the chocolate. Run a fork spirally round, so that the coloured mixture goes into the white in streaks. If preferred put in alternate spoonsful of the two mixtures, and then run a fork round once. Bake in a moderate oven about one hour.

NAPFKUCHEN WITH CHOCOLATE PIECES

$\frac{1}{2}$ lb butter or margarine
$\frac{1}{2}$ lb sugar

3–4 eggs
$\frac{3}{4}$ lb flour
$\frac{1}{4}$ lb cornflour
$\frac{1}{4}$ lb bitter chocolate, broken into small pieces
1 gill milk
2 teaspoonfuls baking-powder
Pinch of salt
Vanilla flavouring

Cream the butter and gradually beat into it the sugar, salt, vanilla and eggs. Sieve together the flour, cornflour and baking-powder. Stir into the creamed mixture, little at a time, adding milk as necessary. It must be kept fairly stiff so as to hold in position the chocolate pieces, which are added last.

Use a ring tin, well greased with butter and sprinkled with flour. Bake in a moderate oven for about an hour.

SAND CAKE

(This should be kept for two or three days before cutting.)

$\frac{1}{2}$ lb butter
6 oz caster sugar
4 eggs
2 tablespoonfuls rum or arrak
Vanilla flavouring
Grated lemon rind
4 oz flour
4 oz cornflour
1 level teaspoonful baking-powder.

NOTE. Some cooks melt the butter and let it cool before beating. Some warm the eggs slightly while beating. An old-fashioned cook without an electric mixer, expects to beat a sand cake by hand for half an hour.

Cream the butter, sugar, vanilla or lemon rind until it is foamy. Beat in the eggs, one at a time and the salt. Sieve together the flour, cornflour and baking-powder and beat this into the rest, adding a very little at a time, and beating vigorously.

Use a long tin, as for a tin loaf. Line it with grease-proof paper,

which has been greased on both sides, and lightly floured before the cake mixture goes in. Bake in a slow oven for 1½ hours.
The cake should be allowed to cool before icing.

ICING

5 oz icing sugar ⎫
2 oz cocoa powder ⎬ sieved together
1 oz cocoa butter ⎭

Melt the cocoa butter. With a little hot water stir the mixed sugar and cocoa powder into a thick paste. Stir in the melted cocoa butter and work in quickly the icing sugar. If liked, paint the cake first with marmalade or apricot jam, liquefied by heating.

GUGLHUPF

This is traditionally served when guests come in for coffee.
In Austria and South Germany, a yeast dough is used and with the addition of lemon rind flavouring, chopped candied peel, chopped nuts, raisins, sultanas, a rather plain, dry, bread-like cake results.
However in German Switzerland, and other parts of Germany a sponge variety is made.

4 oz butter
6 oz sugar
4 eggs
3 gills milk
1 lb flour
2 heaped teaspoonfuls baking-powder
Grated rind of half a lemon

Cream the butter, adding sugar and egg yolks gradually—taking up to 25 minutes over the whole process. Then add the grated lemon and little by little the flour, into which the baking-powder has been thoroughly sieved. Finally fold in the stiffly-beaten egg whites. The guglhupf tin is larger and deeper than the tin for napf kuchen, rather like a pudding mould.

Poppy seeds are made into a filling for a variety of cakes, and guglhupf is one of them.

Take 4 oz well-pounded poppy seeds, 2 oz of sugar, 2 small cups of milk and either 2 oz ground almonds, or almond flavouring. Boil the milk and pour it over the other ingredients, mixing them into a paste. Put alternate layers of the sponge mixture and poppy seed paste into a well-greased tin. Bake in a moderate oven for just under an hour.

Although our rich Christmas cake is known in Germany, where it is called 'English Cake', the native German Christmas cakes are much plainer and simpler. Here are two of them:—*Stollen*, for which there is no translation, so we will call it Bun Cake, as it bears some resemblance to our Bun Loaf, and *Konigskuchen*— Kings' Cake.

STOLLEN (Bun Cake)

(This can be made from a yeast dough. Here is a baking-powder recipe which is quicker.).

> 1 *lb flour*
> 6 *oz sugar*
> 5 *oz butter or margarine*
> 2 *eggs*
> 6 *oz raisins*
> 1½ *oz suet*
> 2 *teaspoonfuls baking-powder*
> 4 *oz finely sliced citron peel*
> ½ *lb dry cheese curd*
> 3 *oz almonds (blanched and cut into fine slivers)*
> 4 *oz currants*
> *Pinch of salt*
> 1 *teaspoonful grated lemon rind*
> 1 *teaspoonful cinnamon*

Well wash and thoroughly dry the raisins and currants and dust them with flour. Sieve together flour and baking-powder on to a pastry board and with a spoon arrange the flour in a ring. In the middle put the curd, which has been rubbed through a sieve, the sugar, the dried fruits and peel and the various flavourings and the almonds. Lastly add the finely chopped suet and the butter. Using the hands, rub and knead together as if making a dough. If the butter is hard, cut it into shavings with a sharp knife so as to make it blend more quickly.

On a floured board form the mixture into a long, flat loaf. Bake in a well-greased tin, in a moderate oven for an hour and ten minutes or thereabouts.

While the cake is still hot, paint it with melted butter and sprinkle thickly with icing sugar.

KINGS' CAKE

(So called because it was originally made for the feast of the Three Kings.)

> ½ lb butter or margarine
> 11 oz flour
> 5 oz cornflour
> 7 oz sugar
> 2 teaspoonfuls baking-powder
> 4 eggs
> 1 gill milk
> 4 oz each sultanas and currants
> 4 tablespoonfuls rum
> Pinch salt
> 1½ oz candied citron peel
> Vanilla flavouring

Well wash the currants and sultanas. Dry thoroughly and dust with flour. Sieve together flour, cornflour and baking powder. Cream the butter, and gradually beat in the whole eggs, the sugar, salt and vanilla flavouring. Then beat in alternately, a little flour and a little milk. Finally the rum, finely-cut peel and the fruit. The mixture should be loose enough to run slowly off a spoon. Line a long, bread-type tin with well-greased paper. Bake in a moderate oven about 1¼ hours.

This cake keeps well in a tightly-covered tin, and is best eaten after a few days.

Short Pastry

The English cook who has 'a light hand with pastry' knows that the secret lies in keeping all ingredients as cold as possible, using enough fat for shortening, working as quickly as possible, handling as little as possible—and correct oven temperature. Exactly the same rules apply to German pastry. If enough fat is used, baking-powder is not necessary, but if you want to economise on fat, you will need a little baking-powder. Always sieve this thoroughly into the flour, and do not wet until the last moment before putting into the oven. *Never* use warm fat. It should be hard enough to be cut into the flour with a knife.

If you have naturally cool hands you can then rub the shavings of fat into the flour—if not—persevere with the knife.

If, despite all precautions, your pastry is sticky, meaning you have added too much liquid, stand it in as cold a place as you have available and dust a little more flour into the mixture. When rolling out, put as little pressure as possible.

Remember that if you are lining a tin, or plate with pastry, it must be well pricked with a fork before going into the oven, otherwise, air-bubbles will form in the pastry.

Short pastry should go into a pre-heated oven, as soon as possible after being wetted.

German cooks almost invariably put an egg in short pastry. Here are three sets of quantities.

1.

½ lb flour
1 level teaspoonful baking-powder
2½–3 oz sugar
1–2 eggs
1–2 tablespoonfuls cream
2½–3 oz butter or margarine
Lemon (or vanilla flavouring)

2.

½ lb flour
1 level teaspoonful baking-powder
1 egg
2½–3 oz sugar
4½ oz butter or margarine
3–4 tablespoonfuls milk
Pinch of salt
Lemon flavouring

3.

½ lb flour
Pinch of baking powder
7 oz butter or margarine
1 egg
Pinch of salt
Lemon flavouring

For Fruit Flans, use a plainer mixture, as follows:—

½ lb flour
2 good teaspoonfuls baking-powder
1 egg
Grated rind of half a lemon

1 egg (save a little of the yolk)—for glazing
1½–2 oz butter or margarine
2 oz sugar
4 tablespoonfuls milk or water

Method (for Flan Pastry).

Sieve flour and baking-powder onto a pastry board. Make a hollow in the middle, and in the hollow put sugar, flavouring, the egg white and most of the yolk, add milk or water, and, using some of the flour, stir the lot into a thick dough. Knife the cold, shredded butter, and the rest of the flour into the dough, kneading with the hands only very briefly to finish the mixing. Let the mixture stand for 30 minutes and roll out lightly before lining the tin. Bake about 30 minutes in a hot oven.

CHEESE CAKE

Pastry:

> 11 oz flour
> 3½ oz butter
> 3½ oz sugar
> 1 egg
> 2 level teaspoonfuls baking-powder
> Pinch of salt

Filling:

> 1½ lb cheese curd
> 3 eggs (separated)
> 5 oz sugar
> Vanilla flavouring
> 1½ oz butter
> 1 cup sour milk
> 1 teaspoonful baking-powder
> 1½ oz cornflour
> Juice and grated rind of half a lemon
> 1½ oz chopped almonds
> 6 oz raisins or sultanas

Make a short pastry and line a spring-mould with it, greasing the tin well first. Put the curd through a sieve, and beat with the sugar and egg yolks until light and fluffy. Stir in the remaining ingredients with the exception of the almonds. Finally fold in the stiffly-beaten egg whites. Put the mixture into the pastry-lined mould, stroking it into a pyramid. It will flatten evenly this way, otherwise it tends to fall in the middle, and sprinkle all over with the chopped almonds. Bake in a medium oven about an hour. When done, turn off the heat and open the oven door, leaving the cake to cool gradually. It is essential not to shake it, or let it stand in a draught until it is completely cold, or it will fall in.

APPLE CAKE

4–5 *oz flour*
3½ *oz cornflour*
Pinch of baking-powder
4 *oz sugar*
2 *egg yolks*
Grated lemon peel
3½ *oz butter or margarine*
1 *lb cooking apples*
1½ *oz raisins*
Vanilla flavouring

Sieve the two flours and the baking-powder onto a pastry board. Make a hollow in the middle and in it mix egg yolks, sugar, lemon peel and vanilla. See that the butter is cold and hard, and flake it on to the mixture with a sharp knife. Quickly work all ingredients together with the fingers, as quickly and lightly as possible. Leave to stand for half an hour in a cold place. Roll lightly and line a greased spring mould with the pastry. Prick the bottom well with a fork, and sprinkle with dried breadcrumbs. Peel and core the apples, and slice them thinly onto the pastry, making alternate layers of apple and raisins, sprinkling with a little sugar if the apples are very tart.

Bake in a hot oven about 40 to 45 minutes, and as soon as lifted out of the oven, sprinkle thickly with sugar, caster or icing.

A variant of this filling is to mix ½ lb cheese curd, 3½ oz sugar,

1 egg yolk, 1 oz cornflour, 1 oz raisins and grated lemon rind, as in the Cheese Cake recipe, folding in the stiffly-beaten eggs whites last, and make a design in the tin by using alternate tablespoons of grated apple, and the cheese mixture. If you like almonds, sprinkle them chopped, on the top and bake in a medium oven for 40 minutes.

LINZ TART

$\frac{1}{4}$ lb butter or margarine
$\frac{1}{4}$ lb sugar
$\frac{1}{4}$ lb each flour and cornflour
Pinch baking-powder
Grated rind of half a lemon
1 tablespoonful rum
3 eggs
Marmalade

Keeping back some of the egg yolk for glazing, beat well together, egg, butter, sugar, rum and lemon rind. Sieve together the two flours and the baking-powder, and quickly rub into the creamed mixture to make a dough. Keep back one third of this. Line bottom and sides of a greased flan tin with the rolled-out pastry, and spread thickly with marmalade. Cut the rest of the pastry into fine strips, and lay them criss-cross over the marmalade to make a trellis. Paint the trellis with the rest of the egg yolk, and bake in a moderate oven 45 minutes.

Flaky Pastry

In preparing flaky pastry, cold is even more necessary, so wash hands in cold water several times while handling. If you have a glass or pastry board, so much the better. Do not handle the pastry more than you must to blend the ingredients. Always roll in one direction, not back and forth, and do not press too hard on the rolling-pin. Any remnants should be laid on top of each other and gently rolled.

The baking tin should not be greased, but wet, with cold water. It is a good idea to have a dish of water at the bottom of the oven, which must be pre-heated and very hot when the pastry goes in. Do not open the oven door for at least fifteen minutes.

Flaky pastry can be cut and twisted into all kinds of shapes, and glazed or iced, or folded into square, or triangular envelopes containing jam or a fruit filling.

As it contains no sugar it is suitable for savoury or meat fillings, sausage-rolls, vol au vents, meat pasties, and so on.

$\frac{1}{2}$ *lb flour*

$\frac{1}{2}$ *lb butter or margarine*

$\frac{1}{2}$ *teaspoonful table salt*

6 *tablespoonfuls water, or skimmed milk, or white wine and water or vinegar and water*

Sieve the flour onto a cold pastry board. Make a hollow in the middle and put into it the salt and the liquid. Quickly work in the flour, forming the mixture into a ball. Cut this across like a hot-cross bun, cover with a basin, and leave to stand in a cool place, preferably a refrigerator for five minutes. It should be of a consistency that does not stick to the hands. Roll out thinly into a rectangle or square.

The butter, which must be hard, is then rolled out between two sheets of grease-proof paper into a smaller rectangle or square and laid in the centre of the pastry. Fold over two opposite sides of the pastry, so that a long strip is formed. Then fold over the two short ends so that they meet in the middle. Then fold again in half, so that you have a four fold thickness. Leave it once again to stand in a cold place for fifteen minutes. Then roll, always rolling away from you, and pressing as lightly as possible on the rolling-pin—folding and rolling, until you have as many layers as you want. Dust very lightly with flour only when absolutely necessary. Bake in a pre-heated, very hot oven for 20–25 minutes.

CURD FLAKY PASTRY (very rich)

$\frac{1}{4}$ *lb cornflour*

$\frac{1}{4}$ *lb cheese curd*

$\frac{1}{4}$ *lb butter*

Sieve the flour onto a cold pastry board. Rub the curd through a sieve and drop it in tiny pieces all over the flour. Flake the butter onto the mixture with a sharp knife. Cut it all together with a large cooking-knife, as for short pastry. Finally, with cold hands, knead and rub together until all the butter and curd is merged. Then roll out as for ordinary flaky pastry. It can be left to stand 2 or 3 days before using, provided it is kept very cool, and is improved by a day in the refrigerator.

Marmalade, apricot jam, or fruit is used as a filling.

Strudel Pastry

This is undoubtedly a job for the expert, but if you are a good pastrycook, and have the right amount of patience and ambition, you will regard it as a challenge to your skill. The dough has to be skin thin, so as to be almost transparent. The texture of the cloth on which it is pressed and rolled out should be clearly seen through the dough. Obviously, to stand this amount of stretching, it must be firm and elastic.

$\frac{1}{2}$ lb flour
8 tablespoonfuls cold water
Pinch of salt
1$\frac{1}{2}$–2 oz butter or margarine
Extra butter or sour cream for glazing
Dried bread crumbs

Sieve the flour. Make a hollow in the middle. Pour in the salted water and mix in some of the flour. Soften, but do not melt the butter, and mix it in, gradually working in the rest of the flour.

Knead this thoroughly on the pastry board until it is firm and elastic, and smooth. Cover with a warmed dish and leave to stand for half an hour.

Then roll out the dough on a floured board. Lay it on a well-floured white cloth and, very carefully, work it with the flat of the hands, pressing outwards towards the edges of the cloth, until it is so thin as to be transparent. Cut off any thick bits round the edge. They can be used in soup.

When you are satisfied you cannot get it any thinner, sprinkle thinly with dried bread crumbs, and then spread on the filling. The dough is then carefully rolled over and over, using the cloth to lift and roll. When the roll is complete, seal it carefully by wetting the edges and pressing together. Flatten slightly with the flat of the hand.

Slide onto a greased baking tin. Paint with melted butter and bake in a moderate oven for about $\frac{3}{4}$ hour.

In South Germany they use rather less butter—barely $\frac{1}{2}$ oz. to $\frac{1}{2}$ lb flour, and add 1 egg.

Strudel Fillings

APPLES

Peel, core and finely slice the apples. Spread over the dough with a handful of well-washed, and well-dried raisins or sultanas and a sprinkling of ground nuts. Sprinkle well with sugar, and a dusting of cinnamon. Roll up and seal.

Instead of apples, stoned and sweetened cherries, blackcurrants, rhubarb, ground nuts, can be used.

CHOCOLATE FILLING

3 oz grated bitter chocolate	1½ oz ground almonds
1½ oz butter or margarine	Sugar and vanilla flavouring to taste
1 egg yolk	

Separate the eggs. Cream the butter, chocolate (warmed), sugar and egg yolk. Add the ground almonds and finally the stiffly-beaten egg white. Spread this mixture on the dough, and roll as before.

Torte or Layer Cakes

The sponge used for these is a biscuit sponge, relying on eggs, and a very little baking powder. Little or no fat is used. A mechanical beater is very desirable to achieve the required degree of creaminess, otherwise the amount of beating needed is likely to cripple the cook.

Have all your ingredients prepared beforehand, i.e. blanch and grind nuts, wash and dry fruit, and line your baking tin. Break each egg in a cup before beating, to make quite sure it is fresh, and divide all eggs into yolks and whites before beginning the actual mixing.

Cakes which are going to be filled with cream should be allowed to stand for twenty-four hours after baking, before any attempt is made to cut them for layering. A large knife (larger than the cake) is needed to cut the layers. Some cooks prefer a very fine wire, like grocers used to use for cutting cheese. After cutting, each slice is carefully slid onto greaseproof paper, and when the filling has been spread on the layer beneath, carefully slide back on top. Some cooks like a layer of short pastry at the bottom of the tin as a base. For baking a spring-mould is a very great advantage, and the mixture must go into the oven the moment the egg whites have been folded in, and it must go into a pre-heated oven that is not too hot. Cool the cake on a wire tray, and be very careful, no jolting, no tilting, and no draughts. Do not open the oven door until the cake has been in for at least 15 minutes.

The bottom of the tin is lined with grease-proof paper, cut to exactly the same size and the top surface of the paper also greased. The sides of the tin or mould are neither greased nor paper-lined, but when baked, carefully loosen all round the sides with a sharp knife. When the sponge is cooked the slight rise in the middle is levelled off with a sharp knife, or wire-cutter.

It is not a good idea to try to economise on the ingredients of this type of cake. If you do, the result will not justify the amount of time and trouble it costs. *Torten* are showpieces for a skilled cook. Unless you really enjoy this kind of baking—better buy your *Torten* in slices at the nearest continental *patisserie*.

BISCUIT SPONGE MIXTURE

3 eggs
3 tablespoonfuls hot water
¼ lb powdered sugar
¼ lb flour (or 2 oz flour and 3 oz cornflour)
1 teaspoonful baking-powder
Pinch of salt
Grated lemon rind

Sieve the flour, cornflour, salt and baking-powder together. Use a clean dry, earthenware or porcelain mixing bowl (or glass) and in it beat the egg yolks, the hot water, and half the sugar to a thick foamy cream. Beat the egg whites into a very stiff mass, adding little by little, the rest of the sugar.

Stir the flour into the egg whites as quickly and lightly as possible and fold the resulting mixture quickly into the eggs. Add the lemon rind, and put at once into the prepared baking tin, preferably a spring-mould.

Bake until golden, 25–35 minutes in a moderate oven. Do not open oven door for at least fifteen minutes, and always close it *very* gently—no jolts.

Another Method

(This is kept warm during beating, and results in a finer textured sponge.)
>   4 *eggs*
>   4 *oz flour and cornflour (2 oz of each)*
>   3½ *oz powdered sugar*
>   1 *teaspoonful grated lemon peel*
>   3½ *oz butter*

Over very low heat, or in a water bath over hot water beat the eggs and sugar to a fluffy mass. Remove from heat and go on beating until the mixture is cool. Liquefy the butter but let it cool before beating in. Finally carefully fold in the sieved flour, and the lemon peel.

Bake in a moderate oven for 30–35 minutes.

A third Method

>   4½ *oz powdered sugar*
>   8 *eggs*
>   3 *oz flour*
>   3 *oz potato flour*
>   *Pinch salt*
>   *Grated rind of half a lemon*
>   *Good pinch of baking-powder*

Sieve together the flours and the baking-powder. Beat sugar and egg yolks to a foam. Stir in flour, and finally very stiffly-beaten egg whites and lemon rind. Bake in a moderate oven 30–35 minutes.

Fillings for Torten

MOCK WHIPPED CREAM

1 *cup sugar*
1 *egg white*
1 *cup fruit juice (from stewed fruit)*

Beat these ingredients together in a glass or earthenware bowl until they are so stiff that you can make a hole with a spoon, which does not fill up again.

BUTTER CREAM

(to which various flavourings, vanilla, mocha, coffee, lemon, can be added.)

4 *oz butter*
2½ *oz icing sugar*
2 *egg yolks*
3½ *oz icing sugar*
1½ *oz cocoa butter*

Cream the butter and the smaller quantity of sugar until light and fluffy. Cream the egg yolks and the larger quantity of sugar until the mixture is almost white.

Then carefully blend the two mixtures and beat for half an hour—five minutes in an electrical mixer. Finally beat in the melted and cooled cocoa butter and any chosen flavouring.

BUTTER CREAM (Another method)

3 gills milk
1½ oz sugar
1½ oz cornflour
2 eggs
2½–3 oz butter
1½ oz cocoa butter
½ a vanilla pod

Boil the milk with the sugar and the vanilla pod, having first taken a little of the cold milk to mix the cornflour to a smooth paste. Beat the cornflour paste into the hot milk, and, when it has cooled somewhat, beat in the two egg yolks, one at a time. Finally fold in the stiffly-beaten egg whites.

Stand the mixture to cool, but stir from time to time to prevent the formation of a skin.

Cream the butter and melt the cocoa-butter. Stirring continuously add the cooled mixture a spoonful at a time, and the cocoa butter drop by drop.

CHOCOLATE BUTTER CREAM

Same quantities as for Butter Cream (Another method), but add to the boiled milk and sugar 1 heaped tablespoon of cocoa, or two heaped tablespoons of grated chocolate.

COFFEE BUTTER CREAM

As above, but add 2–3 tablespoonfuls of strong black coffee.

SACHER TORTE

There are numberless recipes for this famous cake, the speciality of the renowned Sacher Hotel in Vienna. The original is still the secret of the Sacher family.

3 oz butter
3 oz caster sugar
3 separated eggs
3 oz bitter chocolate
3 oz flour

Beat the butter until light and foamy, and then little by little, and alternately, beat in the sugar and the egg yolks, keeping back 2-3 tablespoonfuls of the sugar. Go on beating until the mixture is really light and fluffy. Then beat the egg whites until very stiff and then mix in the rest of the sugar. The mass should be so fluffy that it can be separated with a spoon and remain separated. Fold this, and the sieved flour into the creamed chocolate mixture. Have in readiness a spring-mould, with greaseproof paper cut to the exact size on the base. The sides do not need to be greased. Put in a pre-heated moderate oven, and bake 45 minutes to one hour. Let it cool thoroughly, preferably overnight.

Cut carefully with a sharp knife, or a fine wire, into as many slices as you think the depth of the cake will stand. Spread each thinly with apricot jam, replacing each layer on top of the one below, by sliding it off a piece of grease-proof paper.

Cover the cake with a chocolate icing made as follows:—

CHOCOLATE ICING

½ lb good plain cooking chocolate
4-5 tablespoonfuls water
Piece of butter the size of a walnut

Break the chocolate into small pieces and melt it in the water over gentle heat. Do not let it boil. Stir in the butter, and ice the cake with it while still warm. Stand to cool out of any draughts.

ORANGE CREAM TORTE

Make the cake using whichever method you prefer of the three, see *Torte or Layer Cakes*.

    1 oz cornflour
    8 tablespoonfuls white wine
    Juice of 2 oranges
    Juice of half a lemon
    Grated rind of half an orange
    7 oz caster sugar
    4 eggs
    3 gills cream
    Slices of fresh orange

Stir the cornflour into the wine. Then stir in the fruit juices and the rind, the sugar and the egg yolks. Over gentle heat, preferably in a water-bath, beat this mixture into a thick cream. When it has cooled, beat in the stiffly-beaten egg whites, and the stiffly-beaten cream.

Ice the cake with an orange-flavoured icing. Lay slices of fresh orange on top of the icing, and spread another very thin layer of icing over them.

Orange Icing:
    5 oz icing sugar
    A little orange juice
    A few drops hot water

Blend these to the desired thickness.

STRAWBERRY TORTE

Make your sponge according to your favourite recipe, and allow to stand until the next day. Slice through, and spread each slice thickly with whipped cream in which well-sugared half-strawberries (wild strawberries if you can get them) are embedded. Then cover the whole cake with sweetened, whipped cream, or butter cream—decorate with strawberries, and keep in the refrigerator until brought to table.

All Torten are decorated with elaborate cream swirls. If you have no icing set, make a funnel of two thicknesses of greaseproof paper, secure it with a few bits of cellophane tape, and squeeze the cream through the nozzle end.

The Best of
Scandinavian Cooking

KERSTIN SIMON LONDON

Abbey Library
LONDON

Introduction

The outstanding feature in Scandinavian cooking is no doubt the 'Smörgåsbord'. It is the great show-piece of the tourist trade, as well as the festive treat in traditional home-cooking. Its origin is not quite clear, but it is said to have started long ago with every guest at big country gatherings bringing some kind of food. All dishes were arranged on a long table as a buffet, and the guests helped themselves, starting with bread, butter, all sorts of herring, and cheese. Then they proceeded through smoked, pickled or jellied fish, cold cuts of game, poultry and meat, patés, salads and various hot dishes. The lay-out and garnishing of a real Smörgåsbord is very important. It was meant to be just a first course, and is as such defined in an old encyclopaedia as 'a hindrance to enjoy the main dish if it is a good one, but a reasonable supplement if it is not'. It is also noted that a Smörgåsbord should not be served with an elegant meal. It was mainly used by the Russian and Scandinavian bourgoisie. Cheese taken at the early stage is not a modern idea, but still remains on many Swedish provincial bills-of-fare as a first course called 'Smör, ost och sill'. Butter, cheese and herring.

To-day the Smörgåsbord is seldom laid on in full force at home. Out of the numerous dishes you will find at a proper display in restaurants or on board any Scandinavian passenger ship, each family might have its own abridged version—served at Christmas only, or at very special but informal occasions. It may not look as overwhelmingly lavish and rich as in the public places, but it has a charm and flavour of its own which is difficult to define, but quite unmistakable. The key-word is 'home-made'. You will hardly find anything on the table taken out of tins—if not sardines. It is more likely that even the creamed mushrooms which fill the omelette are hand-picked by your hostess in the woods. Once she has made up her mind to serve a Smörgåsbord she will take tremendous trouble. It is to her a challenge as well as a pleasure. This book will mainly deal with home cooking in this rather old-fashioned style, as opposed to the international instant meal we all know only too well by now. The satisfaction of doing things 'properly', at least once in a while, cannot be overlooked. There is in Scandinavia to-day a very noticeable trend to go back to 'Husmanskost', which means traditional dishes that are economical and simple, but take time and trouble to prepare.

Nearly every item from the Smörgåsbord can be used most successfully as an appetizing first course by itself. Many can be served as the main dish at any everyday meal. The word Smörgåsbord, which is Swedish, is often mistaken for the Danish 'Smörrebröd'. But as the first is served with small variations throughout all the Scandinavian countries, the latter is exclusively Danish. It means open sandwiches, and masterpieces as such. Again each one could be quite a meal in its own right. The buttered slice of bread is always thin, but what is put on top of it is incredibly generous, good, and beautifully arranged.

In Norway the Smörgåsbord is called 'Koldt Bord'—Cold table. In the big hotels at the holiday resorts it is often laid on even for breakfast.

After a good deal of consideration I have decided not to divide this selection of Scandinavian recipes into separate sections for each country. The variations between them are so small that the result would inevitably become monotonous and repetitive.

Smörgåsbord

SVAMPHATTAR—STUFFED MUSHROOMS

Parboil large mushroom hats and marinate for about 1 hour in
French dressing (no sugar, no mustard!). Squash cleaned sardines,
mix them with some grated onion, hardboiled yolk, a suspicion of
Worcestershire sauce and a little mayonnaise. Fill the mushrooms
and serve cold.

Or: Sprinkle them on top with grated cheese and paprika pepper
and place in a greased dish. Put in a hot oven until golden.

FYLLDA TOMATER—STUFFED TOMATOES

Cut a lid off even-sized tomatoes, scoop out the inside, mix it with the same mixture as for the mushrooms, fill the tomatoes and serve cold or hot, as above.

POTTED SHRIMPS

Have no Scandinavian name but are well known. Heat them lightly, take them out of the pot, mix with chopped chives—not too much—lemon juice and a pinch of cayenne pepper. Serve hot on toast, or cold as a cocktail with shredded lettuce.

TONFISKSALLAD—TUNA SALAD

Choose a medium-sized tin of tuna which is *not* preserved with curry. Mix the fish with two hardboiled eggs, diced, 1 tablespoon chopped onion and chopped celery. Arrange on leaves of fresh lettuce and serve with vinaigrette separately, and toast.

LEVERPASTEJ—LIVER PÂTÉ
(Denmark and Sweden)

1½ lb pig's liver	4 fillets of anchovy
5 oz lard	marjoram
2 onions	2 eggs
½ teaspoon black pepper	4½ oz flour (scant)
1 teaspoon white pepper	1 pint of milk (generous), or cream
1 tablespoon salt	3½ oz butter
1 tablespoon sugar	

Put liver and lard through the mincer three times with the onions and the anchovy. (It is easiest to start with the lard.) Season with salt and pepper and sugar; the marjoram is optional. Whisk together eggs, flour and milk or cream. Mix with the liver mixture and add the melted and cooled butter. Put in a well greased cake tin or mould, cover with foil or grease-proof paper. Stand this in a pan of water and bake for just over 1 hour in moderate oven (350 F). Note: for more festive occasions when cream is used it is advisable to sieve the mixture or put it through the liquidiser. The result is an extremely smooth pâté. On the other hand, the flavour will be equally good if one minces only twice—but the pâté will have a rough, farm-house texture which many prefer.

Serve on toast or on ryebread with lettuce as a first course, if not as part of a Smörgåsbord. For one of the most popular Danish open sandwiches: Cover buttered bread with slices of pâté. Garnish with fine jellied stock and pickled cucumber (gherkins) cut into oblong slices. More elaborate, and indeed a meal in its own right: Butter a large slice of bread, brown or white, cover with pâté, garnish with fried bacon and fried mushrooms. Serve with lettuce and tomato.

FIN SMÖRGÅSPASTEJ—FINE LIVER PÂTÉ FOR TOAST

1 lb calves' liver
milk
7 oz butter
7 fl. oz double cream
1 teaspoon salt
2 teaspoons sherry or madeira
(truffles)

Soak the liver in milk for 6 hours. Drain and cut in cubes. Fry lightly, drain again and cool. Mince with the butter. Press through a sieve, or put in a liquidising machine with the cream. Season. (Add the diced truffles with its juice.) Pack the pâté tightly in small containers. Keep in a cool place. They are ready to turn out and serve after 12 hours.

ÄGG À LA LENA—EGGS À LA LENA

1 poached egg for each person. Pâté, tinned consommé, red or green pepper, sherry. Place a slice or a spoonful of pâté at the bottom

of individual cocottes. Put a neatly trimmed poached egg on top. Mix 1 tablespoon of sherry with the consommé and pour around the eggs. Garnish with a ring of pepper. Put in a cold place to set.

'SMÅVARMT'—VARIOUS HOT DISHES FOR THE SMÖRGÅSBORD

A few rather special hot dishes belonged to the old-fashioned family Smörgåsbord. There used to be at least one filled omelette, one kidney-sauté, a dish of chipolata sausages and one or two 'stuvningar'. I have searched in vain for an adequate translation of this word. The nearest is as simple as 'creamed', and can be applied to the two most inevitable ones: mushrooms and sweetbreads. Incidentally, they are excellent complements to each other.

SVAMPSTUVNING—CREAMED MUSHROOMS

Gathering wild mushrooms from the woods is a common and popular pastime in Scandinavia. The knowledge of which varieties to look for is passed on from one generation to the next. The mushrooms were preserved in jars, and a stock of at least a hundred was quite natural for an ordinary household before the disappearance of servants as well as of large larders. Nowadays the findings are either consumed immediately, or cooked and put into the deep-freeze. The same method is used as for the cultivated mushrooms.

> 1 lb mushrooms, cleaned and cut into small cubes or slices
> 1 slice of onion, chopped
> 2–3 tablespoons butter
> 2 teaspoons flour
> 1 pt. cream (double)
> lemon juice
> salt, pepper

Drip a little lemon juice over the mushrooms to preserve their colour. Melt the butter in a saucepan, put in the onion and let sizzle but not brown, just for a minute. Add the mushrooms and fry lightly. Sprinkle with flour and pour the hot cream in the saucepan, stirring. If double cream is used, omit the flour. Let boil, still stirring, until smooth, or about 20 minutes. Add some cold butter and season carefully.

Note: It should not be necessary to rinse the mushrooms. If it has to be done, put them quickly under running water and dry on a clean cloth.

KALVBRÄSS-STUVNING—CREAMED SWEETBREAD

Sweetbreads have been known in Scandinavia for many years as a great delicacy. In Britain they are hardly known at all. The reason might be that the best sweetbreads come from calves, and is rather scarce. When imported—mostly from Holland—it is very expensive. It is, however, very much worth while trying, for special occasions and special guests.—

Clean about 1 lb sweetbread, removing membranes and blood vessels. Soak for an hour in cold water. Put in salted cold water and bring to the boil. Rinse again under running cold water.

Then arrange in a saucepan the following ingredients: a knob of butter, a sliced carrot, a sliced small onion, a bay leaf, a pinch of thyme, some sprigs of parsley and some white peppercorns. Put the sweetbread on this bed, let it sweat for a while on low heat, then cover with water, or preferably veal stock. Season with salt and let boil under a tight-fitting lid about 10 minutes. Remove the sweetbread to a bowl, strain the liquid over it and let cool under light pressure until required, for final cooking. Cut the cold sweetbread in small cubes. Let sweat in a little butter in a saucepan with a thick bottom. Sprinkle with a little flour—let sizzle without browning—add cream, stir and let boil, still stirring, until smooth and thick. If double cream is used, omit the flour. Season with salt, pepper and a suspicion of sherry. Serve as it is, or in a Vol-au-vent, or as a filling of an omelette.

Slice the cold sweetbread, prepared as above. Turn the slices first in beaten egg, then in breadcrumbs seasoned with salt and pepper. Leave to rest for a while on a carving board, then fry slowly in oil mixed with butter. Serve with Petits Pois.

NJUR-SAUTÉ—KIDNEY SAUTÉ

2 calves kidneys (or 8 lambs kidneys)
2 tablespoons butter or marg.
1 tablespoon flour
salt, pepper
1 small jar or tin of mushrooms in water
4 fl. oz cream
consommé or stock
(3 tablespoons madeira or sherry)

Clean the kidneys. Put them in cold, lightly salted water and let boil for a couple of minutes. Rinse them and drain. Cut in cubes or small slices with the mushrooms. Heat the butter in a warm frying-pan. Brown the kidneys lightly and add the mushrooms. Sprinkle seasoning and flour on top. Stir in cream, stock and the mushroom water, season with wine and let boil with a lid on 10-12 minutes.

Note I: If used as a main dish at a family meal, serve with fried potatoes and green beans.

Note II: The kidneys can be made to go further if mixed with leftovers of meat.

PARISERSMÖRGÅS—OPEN SANDWICH PARISIENNE

½ lb best minced beef
1 yolk
2 tablespoons white bread or breadcrumbs softened in a little hot water
1 tablespoon grated onion
2 tablespoons finely chopped pickled beetroot

salt, pepper
large slices of white bread, butter or marg., oil

Mix and beat the force-meat well. Butter the bread and spread it with thick layers of the mixture. Fry in mixed butter and oil, the meat side down first. Be quick—the meat should still be slightly red inside. Serve with capers sprinkled on top, and maybe fried eggs. Garnish with fresh lettuce.

HERRINGS

From all the many herring dishes you might find on a traditional Smörgåsbord I will only include a few which have survived the modern trend of simplification, and are looked upon as minor classics. They are basically the same throughout all the Scandinavian countries, but there might be as many variations of each one as there are cooks and chefs. The salt herring used, comes from the waters round Iceland, and is larger and fatter than any herring caught in the North Sea.

If no 'ordinary' salted herring is available, Matjes-Herring is a good substitute in many cases. They are cured fillets in brine and can be bought in many delicatessen shops or big stores or at the fishmongers, either tinned or not. When the recipe says 'salt' herring it means soaking. That does not apply to the Matjes Herring.

PREPARING DELICATESSEN HERRING

4 lb (generous) salt herrings, rinsed and wiped with paper but not cleaned. 8-9 oz brown or granulated sugar, mixed with 1/3 teaspoon saltpetre. Milk. Put the herrings in an earthenware jar or pot and sprinkle the sugar between layers. Cover with milk and keep in a cool place for three weeks with a lid or a plate on top. Add more milk from time to time, if necessary.

When ready, fillet the herrings and serve with sour cream, chives and potatoes in their skins.

3 *fat salt herrings*

Marinade 1:
    4 *fl. oz distilled white vinegar*
    10 *fl. oz water*
    2 *tablespoons caster sugar*
    1/3 *teaspoon white pepper*
    2 *shallots*
    2 *bayleaves*

Marinade 2:
    3 *fl. oz distilled white vinegar*
    9 *fl. oz water*
    2 *tablespoons caster sugar*
    1/4 *teaspoon white pepper*
    2 *shallots*
    dill
    little juice from pickled beetroot

Soak the herrings in cold water overnight. Then clean, bone, fillet and dry them. (This is a nasty job, and many layers of newsprint should be used on your kitchen table to save it from smelling long after. Have some kitchen paper handy too.) Meanwhile mix water and sugar, and when the sugar is melted add vinegar, bayleaves, pepper and the thinly sliced shallots. Place the fillets in a dish, pour over the liquid and leave in a cool place till next day. When the herring is to be served, take them out and cut them in neat pieces $\frac{1}{2}$ in. thick. Place on a serving dish. Mix the second marinade as the first and pour over. Serve chilled, with hot potatoes.

GLÅSMÄSTARSILL—BOTTLED PICKLED HERRING

4 *large, fat salt herrings*
6 *shallots, sliced*
$\frac{1}{2}$ *carrot*
1 *piece fresh horseradish, sliced*
1 *tablespoon black peppercorns*
3 *tablespoon mustard seed*

3 *bayleaves*
3 *bits whole ginger*

Dressing:
4 *fl. oz distilled white vinegar*
7 *fl. oz water*
4 *fl. oz caster sugar*

Clean the herrings and soak for no more than 12 hours. Scrape them well, but do not skin. Cut off heads, tails and fins, but leave on the bone, Rinse carefully until the water is quite clear. Cut the herrings across in slices just over 1 in. thick. Place them in a glass jar in layers with the onions, the carrot, the horseradish and the spices. Bring the dressing to the boil, leave to cool completely, and pour it over the herring. Cover with a small saucer and leave under slight pressure for 4 to 5 days. Serve from the jar.

SPICKEN SILL—PLAIN SALT HERRING

Top quality salt herrings are required for this very simple dish, which used to be the farm-workers stand-by mid-day meal. Soak the herrings 10-12 hours. Rinse and dry carefully, remove all small bones, and skin. Put the fillets together so that the herrings look whole. Cut in $\frac{3}{4}$ in. slices, place them on a serving dish and garnish with fresh dill—or dried dill seed which now can be found in the big stores all over the country. Serve as the Delicatessen herring with sour cream, chives and potatoes boiled in their skins.

Note: *Matjes Herring* can be served in exactly the same way, as indeed you will find on the menus of all big American hotels in London. But potatoes are not often included or even suggested, probably for slimming reasons. But don't forget them when you try this out at home—they add tremendously to the attraction of the dish.

MATJES HERRING À LA RUSSE

Cover fillets of Matjes Herring with a sauce made of mayonnaise mixed with French mustard, wine vinegar, a little sugar and cream. Put diced hard-boiled eggs, chives, beetroot and capers around them, arranged to give a beautiful colour-effect.

SILL MED BRYNT SMÖR—HERRING IN BROWN BUTTER

Use either Matjes Herring or soaked and cleaned fillets of salt herring. Cover with a mixture of 1 tablespoon diced hard-boiled egg, 1 tablespoon dried dill and 1 tablespoon chopped onion. Immediately before serving, pour over plenty of frizzling, nutty brown butter.

2 big fillets of Matjes Herring 2-3 boiled, cold potatoes
1-2 hard-boiled eggs 4 fl. oz mayonnaise
½ Spanish onion 1 teaspoon curry

Cut the herring in slices and the potatoes in small cubes. Chop the
eggs and onion. The mayonnaise should be fairly thin, but hot with
curry. Mix all ingredients carefully and serve cool.

SILLSALLAD—HERRING SALAD
(DENMARK AND SWEDEN)

2 fillets of soaked, salt herring or Matjes Herring
3-4 boiled cold potatoes
1-2 peeled and cored apples
6-8 pickled baby beets
1 onion
1 small pickled gherkin
juice from the beets, freshly ground white pepper
Garnish: hard-boiled eggs, parsley, grated horseradish (optional)

Dice all ingredients and pack into a mould. Chill for a couple of
hours. Turnout and garnish. Serve with whipped cream, preferably
sour.

SILLGRATÄNG—HERRING AU GRATIN

2 big fillets of Matjes Herring
5-6 boiled potatoes, sliced
2 Spanish onions, sliced
4-5 tablespoons butter or marg.
toasted breadcrumbs

Let the onion-rings sweat but not brown, over low heat in some of
the butter. Cut the herring in small pieces. Butter a shallow, oven-

proof dish very well. Put the potatoes, herring and onions down in layers, beginning and finishing with potatoes. Sprinkle with breadcrumbs and dot with butter, rather generously. Put in a hot oven, or under the grill, for about 10 minutes.

It has often been said that herrings and sprats could be put before Kings and Queens—if only they were more expensive. But they *are* cheap and not appreciated as they deserve to be. The same can be said about the special variety which can only be fished in the Baltic Sea, and is called 'Strömming'. However, once upon a time a famous chef in Stockholm created a fried strömming which soon became even more famous than himself. For many years the recipe remained secret, but it has eventually leaked out. I have found that ordinary herrings and sprats can be treated likewise, with great success.

STRÖMMING À LA OPERAKÄLLAREN—HERRINGS OR SPRATS À LA OPERAKÄLLAREN

Clean and rinse the herrings. To clean sprats, just cut off the head with your thumb-nail from back to front and rip down the middle —the insides will follow. Cut off fins and tails. Salt the fish.
For 1 lb whip 1 egg with 5 fl. oz double cream. Leave the fish to soak in this mixture, for an hour or more. Take them out, keep them well folded and roll in wholemeal flour. Brown them lightly in a hot, dry frying pan on both sides. Then add butter and let them get deep brown.

LÖKSTRÖMMING—ONION SPRATS

2 lb sprats	5 tablespoons sugar
4 fl. oz water	1 tablespoon black pepper
4 fl. oz distilled vinegar	1 teaspoon crushed white pepper
1 large onion, sliced	4 cloves, 2½ tablespoons salt

Mix water and vinegar, and put the sprats in *without cleaning*. Leave for 12 hours and then drain. Put sprats, spices and onion in layers in a pot, cover, and keep in a cool place for 4-5 days. Serve with boiled potatoes in their skins.

ABOUT ANCHOVIES

Many appetizing dishes on the Smörgåsbord are based on tinned anchovy. But what you buy under that name in Scandinavia is quite often something different from the product from Portugal, which you find over here. The fish is slightly larger and fatter, and the unfilleted ones are supposed to be the better buy. They are not preserved in oil, but in a highly spiced brine, mysteriously called lobstersauce or even oystersauce. You may occasionally be able to find this Northern variety in Britain, as the Smörgåsbord gets more and more known. The best place in London is our Church bazaars, always held in the respective parishes in the dark month of November.

SOLÖGA—EYE OF THE SUN

1 yolk
3-4 anchovies, filleted and chopped
1-2 tablespoons chopped onion
2 tablespoons chopped capers
2-3 tablespoons finely chopped, pickled beetroot

Place the anchovies in a ring on a saucer. Outside it a ring of onions, a ring of capers and at the outside the beetroot. Put the yolk carefully in the middle, just before serving so it does not get dry. Mix at the table.

After mixing, the 'Solöga' can be fried quickly in sizzling butter and served at once on toast. Or the mixture can be spread on buttered white bread and put under the grill or in a hot oven for a few minutes.

FÅGELBO—BIRD'S NEST

This is a variation of the Solöga. The same ingredients are used, but diced, cold boiled potatoes are added to the rings.

Yolk as above with rings of anchovy, onion and dill, fresh or dried.

JANSSONS FRESTELSE—JANSSON'S TEMPTATION

This is a hot dish with anchovy, for which Matjes Herring can be substituted. It is often served at the end of a party together with 'the one for the road', and is supposed to tempt the guests to stay still longer. The English either love or loathe it.

5-6 potatoes	2 tablespoons butter or marg.
2 sliced onions	brine to taste
10 anchovies (2 fillets Matjes Herring)	9 fl. oz double cream

Peel the potatoes and cut them in fine strips, like matches. Put these in cold water for a while to get rid of the starch. If not rinsed they might stick together when baked and the dish will be messy. Clean and fillet the anchoy, or cut the Matjes Herring in strips. Fry the onion gently in butter until golden.

Dry the potatoes. Grease an oven proof dish. Put potatoes, anchovy (herring) and onion in layers, beginning and finishing with potatoes. Pour over half the cream and dot with butter. Brown in a moderate oven (about 25 minutes). Pour over the rest of the cream and bake for another 20 minutes, basting with brine, if so wished. Serve from the dish. (4 people.)

KARLSSONS FRESTELSE

As above, but with fillets of buckling instead of anchovy or herring.

BÖCKLING—BUCKLING

The Swedish Buckling looks different and tastes slightly different from what we buy in Britain, due to the fact that the raw fish is the Baltic variety of herring or sprat called 'Strömming'. It is smoked on juniper twigs and has a golden tan like kippers. They are crisp and not yet dry. There is always a variety of dishes with Böckling as main ingredient on the Smörgåsbord, and some can easily and with success be prepared with the British Buckling.

BÖCKLINGSALLAD—BUCKLING SALAD

Strips of cleaned and filleted buckling in sauce vinaigrette (mustard optional) and either of the following mixtures:
Apple, potato, onion. Chives, potato, pickled beetroot.
Shrimps, tomato, radishes, apple, lettuce. Apple, beetroot, potato, herbs.

MARINERAD BÖCKLING—BUCKLING MARINATED

Clean and fillet bucklings, removing as many of the small bones as possible. Arrange in a dish, pour over sauce vinaigrette (no mustard). Leave in a cool place for a couple of hours. Just before serving, sprinkle with chopped dill or chopped chives—fresh if possible, otherwise dried.
Chopped onion can be added to the vinaigrette.

BÖCKLINGLÅDA—BUCKLING PIE

4 bucklings
1 egg
4–5 fl. oz milk or cream
3–1 tablespoon butter or marg.
chopped chives
salt, pepper

Clean and fillet the buckling and put them in a well greased oven proof dish. Whip together egg and milk. Season. Pour the mixture over the buckling and sprinkle with chives. Put in moderate oven about 15 minutes or until set.

4 bucklings
2 hardboiled eggs
1–2 leeks
1–2 tablespoons butter or marg.
2–3 tablespoons double cream
salt, pepper

Clean and fillet the buckling and arrange in a greased oven proof dish. Dice yolks and whites separately. Slice the leeks thinly. Cover the buckling with stripes of green, white and yellow. Sprinkle with salt and pepper and dot with butter. Put the dish in a moderate oven to bake for about 15 minutes, adding the cream after half that time.

Note: Good buckling can be excellent just as it comes, served with scrambled eggs or creamed potatoes.

PRESS-SYLTA—BRAWN

Half a pig's head
1 veal shank
3 ½ pints water
1 bouquet garni, tied in muslin
1 tablespoon crushed white pepper corns
2 tablespoons salt

Mixed spices:

1 teaspoon crushed black pepper corns
1 teaspoon ground ginger
2 tablespoons salt

Scour the pig's head and leave it in plenty of cold water to soak overnight. Put head and shank in a large pot with enough water just to cover. Bring to the boil, skim well and add the seasoning and the bouquet. Let simmer until the meat is tender and falls from the bones. The veal needs less time than the pork and should be removed when ready.

As soon as the pig's head is cooked, remove the rind as whole as possible. Let all the meat cool off, then cut in thin slices. Separate the fat meat from the lean. Strain the liquid, clean the pot and put the liquid back. Wring a cloth in hot water, spread out in a deep bowl and line with the rind. Arrange fat and lean meat in alternate layers, sprinkle the mixed spices in between, and cover with more rind if available. Pull the cloth together and tie securely with string. Put the parcel back in the liquid and let boil 10–15 minutes. Remove it and put in a shallow dish with a plate and a weight on top. Leave in a cool place to set, at least overnight. Serve at the Smörgåsbord garnished with pickled beetroots—or for lunch with fried potatoes, mustard and pickled beetroots.

Soups

SVARTSOPPA MED GARNITYR—BLACK GARNISHED SOUP
(SWEDEN)

This is a very special and elaborate soup which is served at the traditional Goose-feast on the 11th of November. It is very rich and strong in flavour, and not all people like it. This recipe will serve 12–15 people.

> *7 pints veal stock (inclusive stock from giblets)*
> *1 pint 6 fl. oz goose or pig's blood*
> *3 oz flour*

9 fl. oz red wine
6 fl. oz madeira
6 tablespoons brandy
water from boiled apples and prunes.
6 tablespoons vinegar
6½ tablespoons syrup
½ teaspoon white pepper
1½ teaspoon black pepper
2½ teaspoons cinnamon
1 teaspoon ginger
½ teaspoon cloves
5 teaspoons salt

Garnish: slices of apple, prunes, Goose liver Sausage, giblets.

Bring the stock to the boil and thicken with the flour dissolved in some cold water. Boil the stock about 20 minutes. Meanwhile boil slices of apple and prunes in water with a little sugar.

Strain the stock and pour back into saucepan. Strain the blood and add gradually, stirring vigorously. Bring to simmering point, still stirring, and remove immediately from the heat.

Add spices, wine and the water from the fruit. Season very carefully —the soup should neither be too hot in flavour or too sour or too sweet.

The soup will be tastier if cooked several hours, or even 24 hours, before serving. When heated it must be vigorously stirred, or it will break or separate.

GOOSE LIVER SAUSAGE

3¼ oz rice
15 fl. oz milk
1 goose liver or 2 duck's livers
2 oz raisins
1–2 tablespoons syrup
1 slice onion
1 tablespoon butter or marg.

1 egg
1 teaspoon pounded marjoram
salt, white pepper

Boil the rice until next to soft in the milk. (If allowed to get completely soft the sausage will get difficult to carve in neat slices.)
Chop the onion finely and let frizzle in the butter without browning.
Mince the liver and mix with the beaten egg and the cold rice.
Rinse the raisins in hot water and mix into the paste. Add at the same time onion and seasoning. Taste carefully.
Fill the paste into casing or into the skin from the goose's throat. Only fill ⅔, otherwise the sausages will easily break when boiled. Stitch carefully. Prick the sausages and boil with the rest of the giblets without a lid about 45 minutes. The sausages must be completely cold when carved.

GIBLETS

Scald and rinse the goose head, remove windpipe and gullet and pull off the skin. Trim the wing-tips, cut the heart in halves, cut the stomach lengthwise, empty, rinse, and remove the thick membrane. Leave all in salted water until the following day.
Boil in 1¾ pints water with 1 tablespoon salt, some white peppercorns, a couple of cloves and a slice of onion. Remove the giblets bit by bit when tender, and cool. Strain the liquid and let cool. Skim and use in the Black soup.

FISKESUPPE—FISH SOUP I
(NORWAY)

1 lb fishbones, heads (without the gills) and fins
salt, 6 black peppercorns and 4 white
bayleaf, sprig of parsley
1 small onion stuck with 2 cloves (a couple of small carrots)
1 oz butter or marg., 1 oz flour
½ pint milk
2 tablespoons sour cream, juice from half a lemon (sugar)

Garnish:

chopped parsley

Cover the fishbones and etceteras with cold water. Simmer for half an hour with onion, bayleaf, salt and peppercorns, parsley, and carrots if you wish. Skim if necessary. Strain. Melt the butter in a saucepan and stir in the flour. Gradually add about 1 pint of the fish stock, and the milk. Simmer again for about five minutes. Add the sour cream and lemon juice. Season well—some people like a pinch of sugar. Sprinkle with chopped parsley when serving.

FISKSOPPA—FISH SOUP II
(SWEDEN)

1½ lb small fish, for instance whiting or perch, gilled and roughly cut up. 1 sliced onion, salt, some white peppercorns. Water to cover well.
Boil for half an hour. Strain and throw away the fish.
To make the soup:

> *Oil or butter*
> *2 large, diced onions*
> *1 packet saffron*
> *1 leek*
> *parsley*
> *1 small tin mushrooms in water*
> *1 small tin non-seasoned tomatoes*
> *2 small tins mussels in water*
> *1–2 small tins shrimps or prawns*

For 3½ pints fish stock:

> *1 teaspoon rosemary*
> *1 teaspoon basil*
> *1 clove garlic*

Let the onions soften in the oil or butter. Pound the saffron with 2 teaspoons salt. Let simmer with the onions and add the herbs. Strain the water away from all tins except the mushrooms, which is added at once to the saucepan with the tomatoes. Cut the leek into rings and add. Let boil while the mussels are being trimmed. The shrimps or prawns and the mussels are added at the last moment as they should not boil but just get hot.

This soup is thin and delicious and resembles Bouillabaisse. Serve with French loaves and cheese.

OSTSOPPA—CHEESE SOUP
(SWEDEN)

2 pints veal or chicken stock (approx.)
(2 tablespoons dry white wine)
2 yolks
3½ oz grated cheese
5 fl. oz double cream
1½ tablespoon butter or marg.
1½ tablespoon flour
chopped parsley and chevril
salt, paprika pepper

Frizzle butter and flour and add the stock gradually. Let boil 10 minutes, season with salt, paprika and white wine if desired.

Beat the double cream well, add yolks and cheese. Pour the boiling soup over, stirring. The blend should be frothy but not too thick. Serve very hot with the chopped herbs separately. For special occasions, make the following delicious garnish.

ÄGGKULOR—EGG BALLS

Hardboil 3 eggs and let cool in cold water. Cut in halves and remove the yolks. Mix them with 1 oz soft butter to a smooth paste and season with salt and paprika. Put in a cool place to set. Form with two wooden spoons small balls and roll them in diced truffles Cut the white in strips.

POTATIS- OCH PURJOLÖKS-SOPPA—POTATO-AND-LEEK SOUP
(SWEDEN)

3 leeks and 6 potatoes in slices or cubes
1¾ pints water
a knob of butter ·
salt, pepper and cubes of toast

Boil potatoes and leeks with the butter and the seasoning until soft and crushed (1 hour). Serve very hot with cubes of toast.

GRÖNSAKSPURÉ—THICK VEGETABLE SOUP
(FINLAND)

Mixed vegetables:

carrots, leeks, parsnip, celery and potatoes
or *solely cauliflower, leeks, artichokes, etc.*

Proceed as follows:
Boil about 1 lb of cleaned, diced vegetables in 1¾ to 2 pints of beef stock. Press through a colander. Frizzle 1 tablespoon butter or marg. with 1-2 tablespoons flour, add the vegetable purée and the stock gradually and let boil 10 minutes. Season. Whisk 2 yolks with 2 fl. oz cream or 2 tablespoons stock. Add this mixture to the soup, stirring vigorously. Finish with a knob of cold butter.
Note: Not-so-fresh-looking (and cheaper) vegs. can be used for this soup.

NJURSOPPA—KIDNEY SOUP
(DENMARK)

Dice a couple of kidneys with onion or/and parsley. Frizzle in 2 tablespoons butter or marg, sprinkle with 1½ tablespoon flour, add

1½ pint beef stock gradually. Let boil 10 minutes. Season. Whisk 1 or 2 eggs in 3 fl. ozs sour double cream and stir into the soup. Pour the soup in the tureen over 1 piece of toast per person.

KALL TOMATSOPPA—COLD TOMATO SOUP
(SWEDEN)

Cut 2 lb tomatoes in halves and boil in just enough water to cover. When tender, press through a colander and cool. Season with salt, pepper, a pinch of sugar, the juice from half a lemon, 1 tablespoon grated onion and 1 teaspoon Worcestershire sauce. Serve iced in cups.

VÅRSOPPA—SPRING SOUP
(SWEDEN)

1 bunch new carrots
1 small cauliflower
12 asparagus or 1 small tin
5-6 oz fresh peas or 1 small packet deep-frozen peas or 1 small tin
4 oz fresh spinach or 1 small packet deep-frozen

2¼ pints consommé or beef stock (cube)
2-3 yolks
3-4 oz double cream
½ bunch radishes
1 tablespoon chopped parsley
½ tablespoon chopped dill
salt

Clean and rinse carrots, cauliflower, asparagus and peas. Boil them in salt water until tender, cut in small pieces and keep warm.

Bring the stock and the vegetable water to the boil. Add the rinsed spinach and let simmer for a couple of minutes. Season.

Heat the tureen and whisk the yolks and the cream together in it. Add the soup, stirring all the time. Add vegetables, parsley, dill and radishes. Serve hot.

NÄSSELKÅL—NETTLE SOUP

½ lb fresh young nettles
2 tablespoons butter or marg.
3 tablespoons flour

2 pints beef stock (approx.)
chopped chives
salt, pepper (or seasoning herbs)

Clean and rinse the nettles carefully. Boil them until tender in lightly salted water (15 minutes). Dice or chop or press through a colander with the chives. Frizzle butter and flour, add beef stock, stirring, and let boil for 10 minutes. Add the nettles and serve with one poached egg in each plate.

SPENATSOPPA—SPINACH SOUP

14 oz fresh spinach or 1 large packet	1¾ pints consommé or beef stock
3 tablespoons butter or marg.	2 tablespoons double cream
3½ tablespoons flour	salt, pepper

Clean and rinse the spinach and let simmer in its own water 4 minutes. Mince. Make the soup as above. Add the spinach. If frozen spinach is used, do not thaw. Season and add the cream at the very last moment. Serve with half a hard-boiled egg and some cocktail sausages in each plate—and use as a main dish.

GULA ÄRTER MED FLÄSK—YELLOW PEAS WITH PORK
(SWEDEN AND FINLAND)

Before the age of deep-frozen foods, peas like other garden products were dried. A special kind called Åkerärter (Field peas) turned yellow—thus the name. This rather substantial dish is still the traditional Thursday supper during the winter, and is always followed by pancakes. It is served to unsuspicious tourists as a special treat, quite often with hot, sweet punch.

15 oz dried yellow peas	2-3 slices onion or leek
3½ pints water	marjoram or ginger
¾ lb boned pork, slightly salted	(salt)

Clean peas and soak overnight in cold water. Next day cook in same water, bringing quickly to boiling point. Remove shells floating on top, put the lid back and repeat this a couple of times. Add pork and desired seasoning. Cover and simmer slowly until pork and peas are tender (about 2 hours). Remove pork, cut in slices and serve separately with mustard. The soup should be very hot.

SKÅNSK KÅLSOPPA—SCANIAN CABBAGE SOUP
(SWEDEN (SKÅNE))

8 oz lean pork, slightly salted
3 pints water
¼ cabbage (10-11 oz)
1 swede

2-3 carrots
3-4 potatoes (10-11 oz)
6 black peppercorns
1 bayleaf
2 tablespoons chopped parsley

Dice the pork and boil it slowly in the water. Rinse the vegetables, cut the cabbage in strips and the rest in slices and add them to the boiling stock. Season. Let simmer until all is tender or 1-1½ hour. Season again, sprinkle the parsley on top and serve very hot.

OXTAIL

Oxtail may be called a typically English dish in almost every cookery-book, but I still find that my ways of preparing it slightly differ from those of my English friends. I have two versions, one more like a stew and the other a soup. The stew is cooked the 'hard' way, the soup is easy and quick. Both are cheap but worth while doing in large quantities. I buy two or three tails, or at least 4 lb, cut and trimmed.

Oxtail stew

Cut off as much fat as possible from the large pieces, which is always more than the butchers will do. Wash and dry the pieces carefully. Roll them in flour, season with salt and pepper. Fry them in half oil, half marg. until brown all over. Place in a large saucepan and cover with cold water. Bring to the boil and skim with great patience; it will take some time. When you are satisfied with the clarity of the liquid, add all sorts of vegetables, cleaned and cut: potatoes, carrots, leeks, onions, celery if available, parsnips. Parsley, bayleaf, black and white peppercorns, one or two cloves. More salt, and water to cover the lot. Let simmer for 2 to 3 hours. Cool quickly and leave overnight.

Next day remove the fat. Heat the stew enough to take out all the oxtail pieces. Press the rest through a colander. Put it all in cast-iron pot from which it can be served and let simmer again until the meat practically falls from the bones. Season again and serve with freshly chopped parsley on top.

Oxtail soup

Prepare the oxtails as above. Put the pieces in a large saucepan and blanch them, i.e. bring them to the boil, skim off the worst scum and then rinse under running cold water until clean. Clean the saucepan and put the pieces back, cover with salted water and bring again to the boil. This time it will need a little more skimming, but the scum that comes to the surface is white, and when taken off some fat is removed at the same time. Now add two beef stock cubes, one cut-up swede, a sliced onion and a bouquet garni. Let simmer 2-3 hours, removing fat if necessary from time to time. Season with freshly ground black pepper, celery salt and Chinese soy. For the last half hour, add slices of new carrots and rings of leeks. Serve in warm soup plates.

Note: We may *call* this dish a soup but still serve it with mashed potatoes. Thus the family may finish the meat and swede but leave you enough gravy to sieve and leave in a cool place overnight. Then remove the fat and you will have a rich but clear jelly—to heat again and serve as consommé with vermicelli.

Fish and Shellfish

I have met very few Englishmen who believe that they are properly fed after eating a meal without meat. Fish is not supposed to be 'proper food', not filling enough. I am convinced that this attitude is due to the lack of imagination and courage on behalf of most cooks. Fish is too often either just grilled, fried or steamed, and served with nothing to garnish or enhance the flavour, but a sprig of parsley and a slice of lemon—or perhaps a dab of tasteless thick white sauce.

In Scandinavia we deal with our fish quite differently. Fish and shellfish obviously go together, but the flavour of fish can also be brought out by dill, parsley, tomatoes, butter, onions and lemon juice; by carrots even, and mushrooms naturally. The fish is nearly always served with new or mashed potatoes, and often with spinach. When fried it is not so often deep-fried as just dipped in egg and breadcrumbs before cooking.

To keep a good fish stock—or Court Bouillon—takes a little trouble, but is well worth while. Everytime you order filleted fish, ask for the bones and the heads. When in season, buy salmon heads for next to nothing. Cover whatever you have collected with water; add a bouquet, a slice of onion or a shallot, a cut-up carrot, and 3 black peppercorns to 10 white ones, a little salt. White wine, which is good for the flavour but bad for the colour, is optional. Boil for 20 minutes (skim if you want perfection), strain and cool. The result is a very good basis for any fish sauce. It can also be kept, more and more concentrated, for boiling or steaming any fish or shellfish for days to come.

Really fresh fish need not be rinsed, they should only be wiped after cleaning. But as most fish in Britain has been travelling for far too long, and is exposed on open slabs to soot, smog and car exhaust, I would advise everyone to rinse, dry and rub their fish with salt and lemon juice; then leave to rest in a cool place for an hour or so before cooking.

OM LAX—ABOUT SALMON

Salmon does deserve a little chapter of its own. Not only is the Scandinavian salmon quality-wise a good challenge to the famous Scotch—there are also so many varied ways of taking care of this excellent product, down to the last bone or fin, which are not practised over here. I have been as shocked as I am pleased to find that for instance salmon heads can be bought for next to nothing in England in the spring. In Scandinavia they are looked upon as a great delicacy, and you have to pay a proper price.

In the old days nobody would dream of buying less than a whole fish, and then make the most of it. For fun I quote a famous Swedish cook-journalist of the Twenties, who recalls how a salmon was dealt with at the beginning of the century in the small country town where he lived with his parents. Incidentally, he was very rude in later life about female cooks. Nevertheless, when he collected his articles about food and cooking into a book, that book was dedicated to his Mother!

Father brought the big fish home, dangling from a stick carried at the other end by the town's one and only villain, who was given a snaps for his trouble. With the stick on the two men's shoulders, the salmon's tail brushed the cobble-stones. Mother proceeded as follows.

Scale the fish and cut off head and tail. Slit from the back, clean and take care of all blood. Cut both sides clean of the back-bone, remove all small bones, rub, but do *not* rinse. Head, tail and fins are put into cold salted water awaiting their time, when they will be boiled with spices and dill. One side is sent away to be smoked, preferably on juniper twigs. This procedure will take a couple of days. Meanwhile you make from the other side the famous 'Gravlax', of which there are many variations.

GRAVLAX—PICKLED SALMON

To pickle salmon was originally a way of preserving the abundance of fish caught in the rivers of North Sweden during spring and early summer. The prefix 'Grav' means grave, the alternative 'Gravad' means buried. Before the age of ice-boxes and refrigerators, the fish was actually put in the cool earth—in a sort of vault reinforced by rocks and with a heavy wooden door or lid. This sort of larder is still used in vast parts of the Northern countries, as well as on the islands in the archipelago. When Mother had a whole side of a salmon to take care of, she put it skin down on an enormous carving-board and wiped it with clean linen. Then she mixed equal amounts of salt, sugar and nitre and rubbed it in with her fingertips. Next the blood was spread over the side and also rubbed in until the fish was scarlet. Then the side was cut in two, a thick bed of prime dill was put on one piece and the other was turned on top.

The whole 'parcel' was placed between two flat earthenware dishes, a damp cloth was tied around, a light weight put on top— and then down to the vault to be forgotten for 12–24 hours. After that it was considered ready to be cut from the skin in thin slices and served with fresh dill, salt, pepper from a mill and new potatoes. But no sauce.

GRAVLAX—MODERN VERSION

Most books tell you to use at least 2 lb middle cut of super salmon. (Incidentally I have tried much smaller pieces, and even the tail end of a grilse, quite successfully.) Clean, scale and wipe dry. Cut away the backbone and pinch out the small ones. Mix equal amounts of salt and sugar—a tablespoon of each should be enough— with no more than $\frac{1}{2}$ teaspoon of salpetre (nitre), which is optional. A few crushed white peppercorns are again optional; some cooks prefer to use the pepper-mill on the table. Rub the two pieces with this mixture. Make a bed in a shallow dish of fresh or dried dill, put in one piece of salmon skin down, cover with more fresh dill and put the other piece on top, skin up, so that the thick part of one piece meets the thin part of the other. Another layer of dill—then cover with a plate, or a board, or foil and put slight pressure on. Keep cool for 10 to 24 hours, turning the whole packet upside down a couple of times.

Cut from the skin and slice thick or thin according to taste (there are two schools). Cut the skin to strips and shake in a hot, dry frying-pan. They will curl crisp. Serve and garnish with heaps of dill, and lemon.

Nowadays gravlax is served with sauce, but not with potatoes. The sauce is a kind of dressing, and again there are two schools, one of which condemn the use of mustard as a deadly sin. Nevertheless, mustard is a part of the most popular version. Mix in a basin 1 tablespoon of the best sweet mustard—the French is more like the Swedish mustard than any English—with 1 tablespoon sugar and 2 tablespoons vinegar. Add slowly 7 fl. oz of oil, stirring steadily. Finally mix with chopped fresh, or dried dill.

GRAVAD MAKRILL—PICKLED MACKEREL

The method is exactly the same as above, but you always cut thin slices and don't use the skin. Served with no sauce, but creamed potatoes. Only absolutely first class fresh fish should be used.

HEMRIMMAD LAX—HOME-SALTED SALMON

Again the method is the same as for Gravlax, but using half the amount more of salt than of sugar. Thin slices, no sauce, creamed potatoes with lots of chopped parsley and dill. This version is my favourite.

Note. The method is, as anyone can see, a very quick and easy one. Still, if you buy Gravlax 'cooked' the price is even higher than that for Smoked salmon. Which is a mystery to which no one knows the answer, as yet.

STEKT RÖDSPÄTTA—FRIED PLAICE
(DENMARK)

Plaice is especially good and fresh in Denmark, the best coming from Fredrikshavn. It is often served with the unusual garnish of pickled cucumber added to the traditional lemon, parsley—fresh or fried—and new potatoes. Browned butter is a must.

Use a whole fish on the bone for each person, or cut into pieces across the bones if the plaice is large. Cut away heads and fins. Skin by loosening the skin at the tail end and roll off round the knife. Rub with lemon and salt and leave for about an hour. Then dip in beaten egg, then in salted breadcrumbs. For 4 tablespoons breadcrumbs 3 teaspoons salt. Fry rather slowly in butter or margarine, mixed with oil. If the fish can be left to rest again in the coating for a while before frying, so much the better.

Note: Cream and oatmeal can be used instead of egg and breadcrumbs. The fish is often served cold, but is then filleted before frying, and garnished with Sauce Tartare or Remoulade.

FISKGRYTA—CASSEROLE OF FISH—PLAICE OR SOLE

For 12 fillets:

> 1 onion, chopped
> 3–4 oz cheese, diced
> 2–3 tomatoes, skinned and diced
> butter, white wine or fresh lemon juice

Rub fillets in salt and lemon and leave them while preparing onion, cheese and tomatoes. Mix these three ingredients and put a little on each fillet, then roll them. You may need a stick. Put the fillets tightly together in a greased oven-proof dish, moisten with wine or lemon juice, dab with butter. If you have some of the mixture left, put that on top, bake in moderate oven for half an hour, and serve straight from the dish.

OM GÄDDA—ABOUT PIKE

This freshwater fish is not as popular in England as it deserves to be, as it has so many treacherous bones in its body. But it has also a most delicious and unusual flavour. In Sweden it is steamed with salt and lemon juice, and then served with melted butter and grated horseradish, with a sprig of parsley in its mouth. Alternatively the butter is mixed with a little of the stock, chopped hard-boiled egg and parsley.

From one of the most original and funny cookery books I have ever come across—it is Finnish—I quote:

> Pike is an ugly and evil fish which we devour gladly. But we always put something into her stomach first. We mix soft butter with chopped onion, parsley, hardboiled eggs and shrimps. Fill her and stitch her, cover her with breadcrumbs and butter, put tomatoes and potatoes around her and put her in the oven to bake. It serves her right.

BENFRI GÄDDA—BONELESS PIKE
(If you are really worried about the long bones try this)

Clean the fish but leave the head and do not scale. Boil in salted
water and leave to cool. Then remove skin and bones, taking your
time, sitting down quietly. Dice. Make a Béchamel sauce using
half stock, half cream. Season with salt, freshly ground pepper and a
suspicion of chevril. Mix with the pike meat and re-heat. Serve
either with new potatoes or in pastry—as a 'Vol-au-vent'. If you
are in a luxurious mood, add mushrooms 'hats'.

HAVANDE GÄDDA—PREGNANT PIKE
(This is a genuine old recipe, and good for a laugh)

Scale the pike and open her up from the back. Clean but leave the
backbone. Put inside her one salted herring, rinsed and cleaned
but not soaked. Stitch the pike, dip her in egg and toasted breadcrumbs and bake her in the oven in a buttered tin. Baste first with a
little water, then with milk. When the fish is ready, place her on a
serving dish. Thicken the gravy with crushed ginger nuts (believe
it or not) and serve the sauce separately.

TORSK OCH MUSSLÖR—COD AND CLAMS IN BISQUE

This very successful dish was invented in an emergency, when
there was only time to thank Heaven for modern ingenuity in the
field of prepared foods. The three main ingredients were frozen,
dried and tinned, and the result was delicious even from a very
prejudiced customer's point of view. This recipe is included for
fun and as an example of international cooking.

>   1 packet frozen Norwegian cod (large)
>   1 bag dried French lobster bisque
>   water or fish stock
>   1 tin minced American clams
>   1 tablespoon fresh cream

Cut up the cod while still frozen. Empty the Bisque powder into a saucepan with ¾ pint water or fish stock, as indicated on the packet. Stir while bringing to the boil, add the fish, bring to the boil again and then simmer until the fish is cooked (about 10 minutes). Add the drained clams, heat up again and add the fresh cream just before serving; with rice or new potatoes. Serves four.

Left-overs, if any: Put in a greased dish, sprinkle with plenty of grated cheese, dot butter on top and put under the grill until sizzling brown.

FISKEPUDDING, FISKFÄRS—FISH PUDDING
(Norway and Sweden)

For a family meal:

1 lb filleted cod or other white fish
4 oz butter
2 oz flour
1 pint milk or thin cream
2 eggs
Salt, pepper, all spice
breadcrumbs

Pass the fish twice through the mincer. Pass it a third time together with the butter. Put in a large bowl and season—¾ tablespoon salt to ¼ teaspoon pepper. Add the flour and the eggs, one at a time. Gradually add the milk, beating well all the time. If the mixture seems to separate, place the bowl over hot water and beat vigorously. To test the firmness, drop a teaspoonful of the mixture into boiling salt water, when it should set as firm as a sponge pudding. (Test also the seasoning.) If too soft, add some more flour or egg-white, if too solid add a little more milk. Grease an oblong cake-tin, sprinkle well with breadcrumbs and three-quarter fill with the mixture. Cover with foil or with greaseproof paper, well tied around the tin. Place in a baking tin containing water and cook in a slow oven for about 1¼ hours. Let rest for 5 minutes before turning out on a hot dish. Serve with shrimp or tomato or mushroom sauce.

Turbot is looked upon in Scandinavia as a great delicacy, and is priced accordingly. Boil it in salted water (1½ tablespoon to 1¾ pints) with slices of onion and lemon. Serve with grated fresh horseradish fried in nutty browned butter, and garnished with fresh lemon and parsley.

GRILLAD FORELL—GRILLED TROUT, MARINATED
(NORWAY)

1 tablespoon chopped onion
1 tablespoon chopped parsley
juice from 1 lemon
1 tablespoon oil
salt and pepper
4 trout

Marinate the fish for a couple of hours. Wipe and put under the grill. Serve with spinach or/and new potatoes.

OM TORSK—ABOUT COD

I have not as yet met an Englishman who does not despise cod, or anyone who would not rather be dead than order or eat it. There is one good reason for this apprehension: the cod on sale at most fishmongers in England to-day is very far from as fresh as it should be. Moreover, very few cooks know that there is a simple trick to rejuvenate a piece of that sad-looking fish. It goes like this: put the cod under the cold water tap and let the water run for one hour. The fish will come out surprisingly firm, and ready to be cooked in any appetizing way.

TORSK PÅ NORSK—NORWEGIAN COD

3 lb cod   3½ pints water   7 oz salt

Cut the cod in slices, just over one inch thick. Put them into boiling salted water and let boil vividly for 5–7 minutes—*not* just simmer, as usual with any other kind of fish. If not to be served immediately, remove from the heavily salted water and keep hot; left in the water the fish will be too salty. Serve with browned butter, chopped hardboiled eggs and parsley.

TORSK MED SKALDJURS-SMAK—COD WITH A (MOCK) FLAVOUR OF SHELLFISH

1½ lb cod fillets	3 tablespoons tomato purée—
2 tablespoons butter or marg.	definitely not ketchup
lots of dill	½ tablespoon salt

Rub the fillets with salt and leave for a while. Put them in layers in a buttered, oven-proof dish with dabs of butter, tomato purée and lots of dill in between. Cover and put in a medium oven 20–25 minutes. Serve hot *or* cold.

TORSKFILÉ À LA WILLY—FILLETS OF COD WILLY

1½ lb fillets of cod	1 large leek
2 tablespoons butter or marg.	½ tablespoon salt
1 tablespoon French mustard	

Butter an oven-proof dish. Arrange the salted fillets in it and spread mustard on top. Sprinkle thinly sliced raw leek on top of that, and pour as much water in the dish as to reach half the height of the fish. Cover with grease-proof paper, and let simmer 20–25 minutes or until tender.

OM ÅL—ABOUT EEL
(FINLAND)

I quote once more my funny Finnish cookery-book:

Take an eel, this ugly snake-fish, and skin it. It will still live. Cut it in pieces—and damn it, it will still jump! Cruelly, we put it in a pot on the stove. It lives. But when we put pieces of calves kidney and calves liver in its stomach, it gets scared and dies. Naturally, we have plenty of browned butter mixed with oil in the pot, and round onions, tomatoes and parsley. Also diced white bread. Everything is browned all round for about 20 minutes, at moderate heat so nothing gets burnt. Then we pour enough white wine into the pot to supply the eel with necessary juice. When we consider the fish ready to serve, we add a glass of Madeira.

UGNSTEKT ÅL—OVEN BAKED EEL

Clean and rinse the eel, but do not skin it. Cut out the back-bone and remove the fins. Wipe the fish and rub with salt and pepper. Put a grid—or if possible, a bed of clean, dry straw—in a large baking tin. Spread out the eel, skin side down, on it. Bake in a hot oven 35–40 minutes. Brush with melted butter if the eel looks dry. Put the eel on a carving board. Cut from the skin in large but thin slices. Garnish with dill. Serve with new potatoes and 'Skarpsås' (see below), or with creamed potatoes.

SKARPSÅS—SHARP SAUCE

1 hardboiled yolk	1½ tablespoon vinegar
1 raw yolk	4 fl. oz double cream
1 teaspoon French mustard	(chopped fresh or dried dill)
4 fl. oz oil	salt, cayenne pepper

Press the hardboiled yolk through a colander and mix with the raw yolk. Stir in the mustard and then the oil little by little, stirring constantly—as for mayonnaise. Season with salt and a pinch of cayenne. Beat the cream lightly and mix cautiously with the sauce. Finally add the dill.

RÖKT LAX—SMOKED SALMON

A visitor to Sweden in spring-time may have a surprise when first offered smoked salmon. The traditional way of serving it—whether as a first course at a formal dinner party or as a main dish—is with creamed spinach and poached eggs. As such it is known as a 'Vår-primör'—an early spring delicacy.

RÖKT ÅL—SMOKED EEL

Eel is more popular in Scandinavia than it seems to be in England, and is cooked in many various ways. The smoked eel on sale looks larger and fatter than the ones we normally find in London. When served, it is either cut in pieces right across the bone, or boned and skinned and finely sliced. It belongs to the Smörgåsbord, but is also often offered as a first course, accompanied by scrambled eggs. This combination seems strange to the English, but when once tried it goes down very well.

GRILLAD RÖKT FISK—GRILLED SMOKED FISH

  $1\frac{1}{2}$ lb smoked trout or mackerel
  oil or melted butter or marg.

Skin the fish and brush with the fat. Brush also the grilling grid. Heat it and cook the fish 4–6 minutes each side. Serve with new or creamed potatoes; scrambled eggs or creamed spinach; or nettles.

BRÄCKT BÖCKLING—FRIED BUCKLING

Clean the fish and remove the skin. Heat a frying pan and lightly brown butter or marg. Fry the fish quickly on both sides. Put on a heated dish and sprinkle with chopped parsley. Serve with new potatoes, scrambled eggs or creamed spinach.

RÖDVINSSÅS TILL RÖKT FISK—RED WINE SAUCE FOR SMOKED FISH

Boil 1 salmon head (well cleaned) in red wine with a bouquet garni. Strain and thicken with 'beurre manié', i.e. a ball of butter and flour kneaded together.

HÄLLEFLUNDRA I OSTSÅS—HALIBUT À LA RAREBIT

Cut thin slices of halibut (or rock cod) and place them in a greased oven-proof dish. Season with salt and pepper and pour over the fish a few drops lemon juice and some melted butter. Put in hot oven for 12–15 minutes.

Sauce: Melt 7 oz diced cheddar cheese with 1 tablespoon butter and 3–4 oz cream over a low flame. Stir until the cheese has melted. Season with salt, cayenne pepper, $\frac{1}{2}$ teaspoon dry mustard and a little diced gherkin. Finally add 1 beaten egg. This sauce can be poured over the fish either before or after baking in the oven.

RESTRÄTT AV FISK OCH VIN—LEFT-OVER DISH OF FISH AND WINE

Quite often you may happen to have some left-over steamed or boiled fish as well as some white wine. And if you have not—this dish is still worth while trying!

Sauce:

2 oz butter
2 oz flour
$8\frac{1}{2}$ oz milk
salt, pepper
1 lb boned, cooked fish

For the 'gratin':

white wine
$1\frac{3}{4}$ oz flour
3 oz breadcrumbs, not coloured
melted butter

First cook the white sauce, which is rather thick. Season with freshly ground pepper. Cut the fish finely and mesh it with a fork. Mix into the sauce and cool. Form round balls of the mixture, about the size of a mandarine. Roll them in the mixed flour and breadcrumbs. Grease an oven-proof dish and place the balls on it. Pour melted butter over them, with care. Be generous. In the bottom of the dish one glass of wine. Put it in the oven to get golden brown.

Note: But for the melted butter and the wine the dish can be prepared in good time before serving.

RÖDSPÄTTA I SARDELLSÅS—PLAICE WITH ANCHOVY

> 2 large plaice or lemon soles
> water, salt, lemon
> 1 small tin of anchovy fillets
> breadcrumbs

Sauce:

> 2 tablespoons butter or marg.
> 2 tablespoons flour
> 5 fl. oz cream
> fish stock, 12–13 fl. oz

Buy the fish on the bone, but skinned both sides. If you don't have a fish-kettle or a shallow saucepan large enough for the fish, ask your fishmonger to cut it in two or three pieces. You can of course buy fillets; but you get much more flavour in the stock if you cook the fish on the bone. To bone it when cooked may take a little time, but is easy when the fish is still hot, and you waste literally nothing.

Rinse the fish and put in enough water to barely cover. Bring to the boil slowly, and lower the heat so that the water never really bubbles. Use a fork to find out when it is cooked—it should be easily loosened from the backbone, and it seldom needs more than 15–20 minutes; when cut about 10. Lift out the fish with a perforated ladle and strain the liquid. Keep it warm for making the sauce. Put the boned fish in a greased oven-proof dish. Make the white sauce by melting the butter, stirring in the flour and adding fish stock and cream gradually. Let simmer for 10 minutes, stirring gradually. Remove from heat and add lemon juice to taste and the diced fillets of anchovy. Season with care—the anchovies might make more salt unnecessary. Pour the sauce over the fish and sprinkle with breadcrumbs. The whole dish can be prepared beforehand and put in a medium hot oven to brown on top.

LAXPUDDING—SALMON AU GRATIN (4 people)
(FINLAND AND SWEDEN)

1 tin salmon or 8 oz salted salmon	2 eggs
3 large potatoes	white pepper (salt, dried
12 fl. oz milk	chopped dill)

If tinned salmon is used, cut it finely and make sure to remove all skin and small bones. If salted salmon is used, soak for a while in mixed milk and water, dry and flake it. Peel the potatoes and slice them, then dry them in a clean cloth. Grease an oven-proof dish and fill it with potatoes and salmon in layers, starting and finishing with potatoes. Season between layers with pepper, dill if available and salt if the salmon is not very salty. Whisk egg and milk together and pour into the dish. Bake in a moderate oven for an hour. Serve with melted butter.

Note: Boiled potatoes can be used, and if so the oven should be a little hotter and the time for baking 30–40 minutes.

In Finland 1 chopped onion is added and breadcrumbs are spread between layers and on top. The dish is called *Lohilaatikko*.

SILLPUDDING—HERRING AU GRATIN

2 salt herrings, filleted and soaked overnight can be used instead of the salmon, and in this case one chopped onion should be added.

Fillets of Matjes herring can also be used. They need not be soaked; and the onion should be omitted. No salt is needed for seasoning.

PUDDING PÅ RÖKT KOLJA—SMOKED HADDOCK AU GRATIN

Proceed as for 'Laxpudding' using smoked haddock instead of tinned salmon, removing skin and bones.

LAXGRYTA—SALMON POT—JÄTKÄN LOHIPOTTI
(FINLAND)

1½ lb of salmon	dill
water	butter

Cut the salmon in equal slices. Put in a flame-proof dish. Sprinkle salt and dried dillweed over them or between layers. Pour over ½ pint boiling water and ½ lb of butter on top. Cover with a lid and simmer slowly, with the lid ajar, until only a little water remains. Serve with new potatoes.

MAKRILLGRYTA—MACKEREL POT

8 fillets of mackerel, cut in 2 to 3 pieces each. 1 thinly sliced lemon, 3 peeled and sliced tomatoes. Salt, pepper. Chopped dill or/and parsley.

Butter a flame-proof casserole. Put fish, lemon and tomatoes in layers, seasoning between. Top with 2 tablespoons butter, sliced or dabbed. Pour over 3 fl. oz water or stock. Simmer with a lid on 20 minutes. Sprinkle with herbs. Serve with spinach.

FISKGRYTA—CASSEROLE OF FISH
(For a lazy lady)

1 large and 1 small packet frozen cod
1 packet frozen petits pois
3 fl. oz rice (approx. 9 oz)

2 teaspoons salt
1–2 teaspoons curry powder
1 small tin tomatoes
the white of 1 leek
1 bayleaf
1 tomato
lemon, parsley (garlic)
9 fl. oz water
dabs of butter or marg.

Butter a flame-proof dish. Rub the half-thawed block of fish with salt and curry. Cut in slices ½ inch thick. Cut the leek in thin rings. Put in layers beginning with the rice—fish, peas, rice, tinned tomatoes, leek. Add bayleaf (and a clove of garlic), the juice from the tomato-tin and the water, dabs of butter.

Put a lid on and simmer on top of the stove or in a slow oven for 30 minutes. Leave to rest but keep it warm for another 5–10 minutes. Garnish with sliced lemon, tomato and chopped parsley.

FISKPUDDING—FISHPIE (OF LEFT-OVERS)

About 1 lb cooked fish, boned and finely cut
4 oz rice, cooked 20 minutes, rinsed with cold water and strained
3½ fl. oz cream, 3½ fl. oz fish stock
a little melted butter, salt, pepper
2 yolks, 2 whites
toasted breadcrumbs
grated cheese
a little more melted butter

Mix in a bowl fish, rice, cream, butter, seasoning, stock and yolks. Beat the whites and fold them into the mixture. Butter an oven-proof dish and sprinkle with breadcrumbs. Pour the mixture into that and sprinkle again on top with breadcrumbs and a generous amount of grated cheese. Finish with melted butter and bake in a moderate oven 30–40 minutes.

RÖDTUNGA MED SPENAT OCH MORÖTTER—LEMON SOLE WITH SPINACH AND CARROTS

4 lemon soles, filleted, ½ pint of stock or white wine, or stock and
*   wine mixed*
1 lb new carrots, water, ½ teaspoon caster sugar
1 lb spinach, fresh, or a packet of non-chopped frozen
*   butter, seasoning*

Cut the carrots in fine slices and boil with the sugar in a little water until soft. Melt the spinach in butter, season with salt, pepper and grated nutmeg. Simmer the fillets 4–5 minutes. Move them carefully with a perforated ladle to the middle of a heated dish. Arrange the carrots on one side of them and the spinach on the other. Whisk all reduced juices together, strain and pour over fish and vegetables

SJÖTUNGA MED OLIVES OCH GRÖNA DRUVOR—DOVER SOLE WITH OLIVES AND GREEN GRAPES

4 dover soles, filleted
1 jar stoned olives (10 fl. oz)
1 lb peeled and seeded grapes
½ pint fish stock
6 fl. oz butter
salt

Cut the olives in rings. Simmer butter and stock in a wide and shallow saucepan. Heat the olives, and then the grapes in this; remove them with a perforated ladle and keep warm. Roll the fillets and fix them with a toothpick, pack them tightly in the saucepan, put a lid on and let simmer 4–5 minutes. Remove them too with a perforated ladle, arrange them in the middle of a heated dish and place the olives on one side and the grapes on the other. Season the juice in the pan, reduce it if necessary, strain and pour into the dish. Serve at once. This is an elegant dish, suitable for a ladies' lunch. Make it even more sophisticated by serving it with chilled cucumber salad.

RYSK KOLJA—HADDOCK À LA RUSSE

1 haddock weighing at least 2 lb
2 tablespoons salt to 2 pints of water
1 onion, 1 bayleaf
3 black peppercorns, 10 white

Boil the fish whole, with head and fins; the liquid should barely cover and barely simmer, and cooking time need be no more than 15 minutes. Bone, and keep warm. Strain the stock, and make a white sauce using the stock and equal amount of top of the milk. Finish it off with dabs of cold butter and 1 yolk. Pour over the fish in a shallow dish. Garnish with lots of chopped fried onion and crushed hard-boiled egg. If necessary, heat in the oven before serving.

SAUCES

With boiled, steamed or baked fish:

SMÄLT SMÖR MED HACKADE ÄGG—BUTTER AND EGG SAUCE

3½ oz butter
2–4 tablespoons fish stock
1 hard boiled egg
1–2 tablespoons chopped parsley

Melt the butter and blend with fish stock. Crush the egg with a spoon and mix with the rest. Season with a little salt to taste.

RÖRD SMÖRSÅS—STIRRED BUTTER SAUCE

3½ oz butter
2 yolks
salt, pepper
1 tablespoon lemon juice

Put butter and yolks[4] in a bowl and stir with a wooden spoon continuously until the butter is creamy and bubbly. Gradually add the lemon juice. Serve immediately.

SENAPSSÅS—MUSTARD SAUCE

1 tablespoon butter
2 tablespoons flour
1 teaspoon dry mustard (scant)
12 fl. oz fish stock, $3\frac{1}{2}$ fl. oz cream

Frizzle butter, flour and mustard in a saucepan. Stir in the hot liquid and let boil 10 minutes.

FALSK HOLLANDÄS—MOCK HOLLANDAISE

2 oz or 2 tablespoons butter
2 yolks
1 tablespoon flour, generous
9 fl. oz fish stock
juice from $\frac{1}{2}$ lemon
salt (sugar) pepper

Half the butter, nearly all the stock, the yolks and the flour are whisked together in a thick-bottomed saucepan. Put over a low flame and bring to simmer but not boil. Everytime the sauce is near boiling, add a dab of cold butter or a drop of cold stock. When all the butter and stock are used and the sauce is thick and creamy, season and serve.

KALAS-SÅS—PARTY-SAUCE

Whisk 10 fl. oz double cream. Stir in 2 yolks, one by one. Flavour with $1\frac{1}{2}$ tablespoon wine vinegar, $1\frac{1}{2}$ tablespoon caster sugar, 1 generous teaspoon French mustard, freshly ground white pepper. Equally good with hot or cold fish.

This requires 'the real thing' again—the biggest and fattest salt herrings you can buy. For 4 people.

    2 salt herrings
    4 tablespoons butter or marg.
    2 tablespoons chopped fresh dill or 2 teaspoons dried dill weed
    2 tablespoons chopped parsley
    2 tablespoons chopped fresh chives, or the green of leeks, or onion

Clean the herrings, fillet, rinse and soak for 8–12 hours. Butter 4 sheets of grease-proof paper. Put one fillet on each and cover with the herbs. Fold to neat parcels and fry slowly on top of the stove or bake in the oven until the paper is browned. Put the parcels on a serving dish and don't unfold until on the plate in front of each person. Serve with potatoes in their skins, boiled or baked.

STEKT SILL MED LÖK—FRIED HERRING WITH ONIONS

This is a century-old dish, loved by the poor and the rich alike, and by tradition most often served on Mondays. In many parts of the countryside the mid-day meal is called breakfast, is served around 11 o'clock and would remind any Englishman of *his* traditional breakfast. This is as common as kippers.

    4 salt herrings
    2 tablespoons butter or marg.
    2 large onions
    2 tablespoons toasted breadcrumbs
    2 tablespoons flour
    top of the milk

Soak the herrings 10–18 hours. Clean, fillet and rinse. Remove small bones. Dry. Put the fillets in a paper or plastic bag with the breadcrumbs and flour mixed. Shake until they are well covered. Peel the onions and cut in slices or rings. Fry them gently until light brown, remove them and keep hot. Fry the fillets in the same fat, arrange them on a hot serving dish with the onions on top. Pour the boiling cream-milk in the frying pan, stir, and pour over the herrings. Serve with potatoes in their jackets.

SILLGRATÄNG PÅ FÄRSK SILL—FRESH HERRING AU GRATIN

6 fresh herrings
White peppercorns, freshly milled
1 medium-sized onion
dried dill
1–2 tablespoons smoked cod roe, mixed with the double amount
*   butter*
breadcrumbs and margarine

Clean and rinse the herrings, remove the bone, and fillet. Put them on a board with the skin-side down and sprinkle with white pepper, finely chopped onion and dried dill-weed. Put a knob of cod-roe-butter on each, roll them and put in a greased oven-proof dish. Breadcrumbs, and small knobs of butter on top. Bake in a hot oven for 15–20 minutes.

TRELLEBORGSGRYTA—HERRING AND TOMATO STEW
(SWEDISH)

Clean and fillet fresh herrings. Roll them and pack them tightly together in a greased and salted oven-proof dish. Mix fresh lemon juice with water and cover the herrings, but only just. Peel a lot of small onions, boil them in salted water for 5 minutes. Dip tomatoes in the same boiling water and peel them. Put the onions and the cut-up tomatoes on top of the herrings, sprinkle with dried dill, chopped parsley, salt and pepper. Dot with knobs of butter, cover and let boil for 20 minutes.

Marinade:

> 1 tablespoon lemon juice
> 1 dessertspoon salt
> 1 dessertspoon dried dill, chives or a little chopped green of leek
> 3 fl. oz oil
> Whisk this with 1–2 tablespoons cheap madeira

Put clean fillets of fresh herring in this marinade and leave them for a couple of hours. Turn them two or three times. Then dip in toasted breadcrumbs. Fry in butter and serve with new potatoes and spinach.

OM HUMMER—ABOUT LOBSTER

It is often said that British Lobster as so many other things are the best in the world. If this is true, it is the more regrettable that the cooked lobster you buy at many fishmongers are so often sadly dry and dirty, and that one has to be suspicious of the clean, moistlooking and appetizing ones. Too often those come out of the freeze, and you can only tell by a certain lightness.

Any ambitious cook could cook lobsters at home. One need not be specially courageous or even feel cruel. Their death is certainly quicker when you cook one or two, then when dozens are done at a time.

They have to be specially ordered. Make sure they are lively, and leave them in the sink—dry!—while you prepare the 'court bouillon'. For two medium sized lobsters, or one large, you need

> 5½ pints water
> 1 oz vinegar
> 1 sliced carrot
> 2–3 slices onion
> 3 tablespoons salt
> ½ bayleaf

some sprigs of parsley
one sprig thyme
8–10 white peppercorns
fresh or dried dill, optional

Boil all these ingredients with the lid on for 30 minutes. Make sure that the lobster is still alive by straightening the tail and hit the end of it. The lobster should then quickly curl it in under himself. Rinse quickly under the running tap with cold water. Tie the claws with thick rubber bands. Put the lobster head first in the boiling water and replace the lid quickly. Small lobster are cooked in 12–15 minutes, medium sized in 15–20 and large in 20–25 minutes. Don't overcook, or the meat will get tough.

Let them get cold in their water. This is where the fishmongers so often fail—they take them out when still warm, and that is why the lobsters are dry. Home-cooked lobsters are delicious as they are, served split with mayonnaise or vinaigrette. They can also be served warm in their court-boullion—one small lobster for each person. Messy but good. Sauce Hollandaise, thinned with the stock, goes well.

SKALDJURSGRYTA MED PIGGVAR—CASSEROLE WITH SHELLFISH AND TURBOT

This dish was 'invented' for an informal 21st birthday dance, when something more original than a cold buffet was asked for by the young host. It is worth trying. For 30 people: About 12 lb filleted turbot—chosen as a basis because it is a firm fish with a distinctive and delicious flavour. 2 live lobsters. 1 large, heavy crab. 6 mediterranean or Dublin prawns. 1 large packet of frozen shrimps. 1 lb button mushrooms.

Bring the turbot to the boil in a large fish kettle with just enough water to cover. To each pint of water 1 scant tablespoon salt. Add 1 small peeled sliced lemon. Skim well. Put on the lid and let it simmer for about 10 minutes, according to the thickness of the fillets. It is important not to overcook turbot. When just ready, remove and drain, and keep covered in a cool place.

Remove the lemon slices and add fresh or dried dill to the stock. Boil the lobsters in this, and let them cool in the stock—maybe overnight.

Remove the meat from the lobsters, the crab and the prawns. Defrost the shrimps. Make a sauce of 4 tablespoons butter, 4 tablespoons flour and 1¾ pint mixed stock and creamy milk. Season well with salt, cayenne pepper, curry to taste (it should not be allowed to dominate, only to give a richer flavour) and allspice (Epice Riche). Thicken the sauce with 2 yolks stirred in 3 fl. oz cream. Finally stir in 2 or 3 knobs of butter.

Heat the fish in a big casserole, heat the shellfish in the sauce and pour over. Garnish with lightly fried mushrooms, serve with a big bowl of hot, dry rice.

HUMMERSTUVNING—LOBSTER STEW

Remove all meat from 1 large lobster and keep covered in a cool place. Pound the shells in a mortar. Add 3 tablespoons butter and go on pounding until the mixture is a smooth paste. Put in a saucepan and let frizzle but not brown. Add enough water as barely to cover. Boil for 15 minutes and strain. Throw the shells away. Let the mixture cool quickly and leave in a cold place until the butter is set on top. Remove carefully and use at once.

For the stew:

> 2–3 tablespoons lobster-butter
> 8 fl. oz cream
> 2 tablespoons flour
> (½–1 tablespoon brandy)
> salt, cayenne pepper, ground cloves
> shell-water from under the butter

Frizzle flour and butter, add cream and shellwater and let boil for 5 minutes. Add the cut meat and season. The brandy will enhance the flavour. Heat, but do not let the meat boil, or it will get tough.

As above, but with more liquid added. If home-cooked lobster is used, the strained bouillon will have enough flavour, and one can do with ordinary butter instead of the specially prepared. If bought lobster is used and there is no time to make lobster-butter, fish-stock as described in the introduction to 'Fish' will do, but the sauce will naturally taste less of lobster.

Note: Both the stew and the sauce can be made less extravagantly if the lobster meat is halved and mixed with equal amount of boiled white fish or fish pudding. Other suggestions are about 5 oz lightly fried mushrooms or 2–3 hard-boiled eggs.

RÄKSÅS—SHRIMP SAUCE

Shrimpshells, well rinsed, can be used to make as above to give more flavour to the sauce.

7 oz shrimps	12 fl. oz fish stock or shell water
2 tablespoons butter or marg.	3 fl. oz cream
2–3 tablespoons flour	dill if available

Dice the shelled shrimps. Frizzle butter and flour, gradually add the liquid and boil stirring, 5–10 minutes. When ready, add the chopped dill.

HUMMER-KOTLETTER—LOBSTER CUTLETS

This recipe is from my oldest cookery-book, published 1879, and written by a doctor famous for his gastronomic skill (I quote from his 'The art of cooking' about pigeons as well). I tried these cutlets years ago for the first time, because I found them so deliciously extravagant and because of the doctor's note: Worthy of attention. Which proved to be an understatement.

3 boiled hen lobsters, butter, 3 eggs, toasted breadcrumbs, 2 dessertspoons 'anchovy-essence' (substitute: crushed anchovy), nutmeg, sugar, pepper, salt, a little flour. The flesh is picked out

of the lobsters and pounded in a mortar with some of the red roe, 2 well beaten yolks, 1 egg-white, 1 spoon anchovy and the spices. (If you have a machine, mince and liquidise.) Blend with a little flour and roll out to a thick cake, from which you cut out cutlets. Dip them in beaten egg, then in breadcrumbs, and fry them light brown in butter. Sauce: melted butter, 1 spoon anchovy and the rest of the roe.

HUMMERSALLAD—LOBSTER SALAD (10 people)

6 lobsters of approx. 1 lb each
2 red peppers
6 lettuces
1 lb mayonnaise
4 fl. oz tomato-ketchup

Take out the tails whole from the shells, remove the intestine and cut the tails in halves lengthwise. Try to keep the claws as whole as possible too. Carefully remove the stomach from the head. Pack all the soft pulp and fat from the shells in a bowl and turn it out on a serving dish. Arrange the tails and the claws standing up around and on top of it. Decorate with the red roe.

Remove the pips from the peppers and cut them into rings and strips. Cut the cleaned and dried lettuce in strips. Place alternate piles of pepper and lettuce round the lobster. Stir the ketchup into the mayonnaise and serve separately.

KRABBGRATIN—CRAB AU GRATIN

1 medium to large crab, or 2 small crabs, or 2 dressed crabs or 1 large tin of crab. Remove all meat from the crabs if they are bought whole. If you use a tin, make sure to get rid of the long hard transparent strips inside the legs and claws. 2 diced apples. Sauce:

2 tablespoons butter or marg.
2 tablespoons flour

½ pint fish stock, juice from the tin
8 fl. oz cream, 1 yolk
salt, cayenne pepper, curry powder
Breadcrumbs, grated cheese, dabs of butter

The apples 'lighten' the somewhat heavy flavour of hot crab. Make a sauce of butter, flour, stock and cream and season carefully with cayenne and curry: a suspicion of cayenne and no more than ½ teaspoon of curry. Add the yolk after removing the saucepan from the flame. Mix in the crab-meat and the apple, put in a shallow buttered dish or in shells, cover with ample grated cheese and toasted breadcrumbs, dab with butter, and put in the oven or under the grill to brown.

KALL KRABBA—COLD CRAB

Serve with mayonnaise or sauce as for 'Gravlax': 1 tablespoon of sweet mustard—the French is more like the Swedish than any English—1 tablespoon castor sugar, 2 tablespoons wine vinegar, 7 fl. oz oil. Chopped fresh or dried dill. This sauce is equally suitable for lobster. Garnish with lettuce.

Meat

The most notable difference about the ways with meat between Britain and Scandinavia might be that we don't make pies, at least not to the same extent. When they are done, they are not much different from the English ones. The Finns call a pie a 'Pirog', and the most common filling is fish, egg and rice. Roast beef is not served with Yorkshire pudding, but with glazed onions and fried potatoes or Pommes Frites. The butchers cut the continental way, and fillet is always available, at a price.

Our lamb is not up to English standard, but our veal is better. Pork is much more common than in Britain, and not looked upon with any suspicion. Elk, venison and reindeer add to the choice during the winter. Elk especially was a godsend during the war. It is very like beef, but tends to be tougher. One of the most delicious dishes I ever tasted was smoked fillet of deer, cooked in wine and served cold, with horseradish in cream and cucumber salad.

The attentive reader will note that garlic is hardly mentioned. Those who like it can add it to many of the receipes, especially the stews. For a mild effect try this trick: crush a clove and rub it with salt, using an ordinary tableknife. Then season with the salt.

When I buy mince I choose the cut I want and then ask the butcher to mince it.

For stock I always whisk out the residues in roasting tin and frying pan with water, reduce it and strain it. Then leave it in a cool place until the fat can be easily removed.

The fat from the bottom of the grill after cooking steaks or chops is poured over the vegs.

A 'bouquet' is parsley, bayleaf and thyme.

SLOTTSTEK—CASTLE ROAST BEEF

The way Scandinavians to-day deal with an 'ordinary' Roast Sirloin does not differ much from the classical English method. But the Yorkshire pudding is hardly known. The joint is served with braised onions and roast potatoes. Quite often a large onion is put in the baking tin to add to the flavour. The gravy is not thickened.

The old-fashioned way of roasting was *quite* different. The following recipe was often used for Sunday dinner, as indeed the few other roasts included in this book.

>   *3 lb sirloin, boned and rolled*
>   *2 tablespoons butter or marg.*
>   *9 fl. oz stock or consommé*
>   *1 onion*
>   *2 fillets of anchovy*

1 *bayleaf*
1 *tablespoon distilled white vinegar*
1 *tablespoon syrup*
1 *tablespoon 'Beurre manié' (equal amount butter and flour kneaded
     to a ball)*
5 *fl. oz cream*
5–7 *white peppercorns, 3–4 black*
salt, pepper

Rub the meat with salt and pepper and brown it all round in a
stewing pan on top of the stove. Add some of the hot stock and
all the rest *except the Beurre manié*. Leave to braise gently and slowly
under cover, turning it from time to time and basting with more
stock when necessary. It can also be put in a medium oven for
roughly 2 hours. Take it out and keep it hot. It should be well done.
Strain the juice and whisk out the residue from the pan with hot
water or stock. Bring the juice to the boil, thicken by adding the
Beurre manié, stirring. Add the cream, bring back to the boil,
still stirring, and season if needed.
Serve with boiled potatoes, cucumber salad, red currant jelly or
cranberry.

LAMMSTEK—ROAST LAMB

The mutton and lamb in Sweden is of poor quality compared to
the British. It is nevertheless looked upon as a delicacy. The saddle
especially is a favourite joint for festive occasions.
There might be a few points worth while noting, and maybe
trying. One thing is that garlic is nearly a 'must'. Either a clove is
inserted next to the bone, or it is crushed with salt and rubbed all
over the joint.
In the old days lamb was basted with white coffee. A more modern
idea is to baste with sherry.
Some books say that the joint should be rubbed with mustard.
Some suggest seasoning the thick gravy with black currant jelly.
(My English family does not believe in any of these suggestions.)

Mint sauce is not known. Mutton or lamb is served with all kinds of vegetable like sprouts, small carrots, peas or/and cauliflower, fried potatoes and quite often cucumber salad, or any other salad.

KALVSTEK—ROAST VEAL

Contrary to lamb, veal is of better quality in Scandinavia than in Britain. Roast veal is a popular Sunday dinner, and very simple. It should be boned and rolled, but not stuffed. Brown it in a tight cast-iron pan on top of the stove. *After* browning, rub with salt and pepper, using the back of a wooden spoon. Baste with hot cream and stock, a little at the time. Braise under cover in a moderate oven—not more than 2 hours for 3 lb. Baste every 20 minutes. Take out when tender and keep hot. Thicken the gravy with 2 teaspoons of arrowroot, dissolved in a little water, and season with nothing but salt. Serve with fried potatoes, cucumber salad, and peas.

JULSKINKA—CHRISTMAS HAM

In the old days it was a common thing to prepare the fresh ham at home. First it was rubbed with salt, sugar and nitre and left in a cool place 1–3 days, turned occasionally. Then left for 3 weeks in a boiled, cold brine made of water and the same ingredients as above. Then it was ready to cook. But light smoking was supposed to enhance the flavour, and thus we come very close to an English gammon.

> *1 gammon of 8½ lb*
> *water*

Coating:

½ *tablespoon mustard*	*3 tablespoons breadcrumbs*
½ *coffeespoon ginger*	½ *tablespoon sugar*

Soak the gammon for 24 hours. Scrape the dark side lightly, wipe and place in a large saucepan, cover with water. Bring to the boil

as quickly as possible, and skim carefully. Then put back the lid
and let simmer on *very* low heat and boil for 4 hours or longer.
Try with a skewer, or better still with a thermometer which
should show 178 F when the ham is ready. Let cool in its liquid as
quickly as possible.

Note: A bouquet garni, 2 onions with 6 cloves stuck into them, a
small piece of nutmeg and a piece of celery put in after the skimming
is done will make the final flavour even better. It is a modern idea.
When the ham is cold pull off the skin. Spread the fat with mustard
and ginger, then the breadcrumbs mixed with sugar. (Garnish with
a few cloves.) Bake in a hot oven to brown quickly. Serve hot or
cold with Cumberland sauce, mashed potatoes and peas. Or—if
you wish to follow the old Swedish tradition for Christmas Eve
try this:

DOPP I GRYTAN—DIP IN THE POT

Strain the liquid, reduce and skim again. Keep it simmering on the
stove. Place beside it sliced white bread and ryebread and let
everyone help themselves, dipping the bread in the liquor, to be
eaten with the ham which is served cold. Mustard is a must.

FLAESKESTEG—ROAST PORK
(DENMARK)

5-6 lb of leg or shoulder of pork (fresh, not smoked or salt)
salt; mustard or ginger
Cloves, bayleaf and onion, optional
water

Pork is the Danish favourite roast. The main attraction is the crisp
crackling. A 'must' to be served with it is red cabbage.
Scrape the rind and score it with a sharp knife in lines about ½ in.
apart, or into squares. (Your butcher might do this for you.) Wipe
the scored pork with a hot, damp cloth. Rub it with salt, and

mustard or ginger. A few cloves, bits of bayleaf and onions can be stuck into the incisions.

Roast 'dry' for a few minutes in a hot oven. Add boiling water and cook for 2–3 hours *without basting* in a moderate oven. Remove the gravy 30 minutes before the joint is ready and finish the roasting with the oven left slightly ajar for the last quarter of an hour.

Strain and skim the gravy. Add a few drops of browning if necessary. Serve as it is, or thicken with 'beurre manié'—flour and butter kneaded into a walnut-sized ball.

The red cabbage is prepared as follows: Melt 2 tablespoons of butter with 6 tablespoons of sugar. Cook on low heat, and don't let the mixture brown. Add a medium-sized shredded cabbage and stir until the liquid has evaporated. Then gradually add 3–4 fl. oz blackcurrant juice or jelly. Simmer until tender, which might take 2–3 hours. Season with salt.

If possible, prepare the day before serving and heat gently when the cabbage is to be used.

PATTEGRIS—SUCKLING PIG

This belongs to the Christmas fare and can be found in England at high class butchers. In Denmark it is put in a very hot oven and browned all round. Then water is added, the heat lowered, and the pig is basted every ten minutes. It is roasted for about 2 hours, with the oven door ajar for the last 10 minutes at maximum heat for the crackling to get crisp. The gravy is thickened with a little flour dissolved in water, and seasoned with mustard and claret.

SURSTEK—SOUR ROAST

4 lb sirloin
3½ oz lard
2 teaspoons mustard
2 tablespoons butter or marg.
salt, pepper

Gravy:

    2 tablespoons fat from the pan
    2 tablespoons flour
    8 fl. oz meat juice
    4 fl. oz hot cream

Marinade:

    1 pint red wine
    4 fl. oz vinegar
    4 fl. oz oil
    4 shallots (small onions)
    a pinch of thyme, 2 cloves
    5 crushed white pepper corns
    1 bayleaf
    1 tablespoon crushed juniper berries
    1 tablespoon sugar
    2 teaspoons salt

Method for marinade: Fry the shallots lightly in the oil. Add all ingredients, bring to the boil and let cool.

Rinse the meat and rub with mustard. Put in the marinade and leave in a cool place 5–10 days, turning it from time to time and making sure it is covered by the liquid.

When wanted, rinse the meat and wipe it dry. Cut the lard in fingers, roll them in salt and pepper and lard the roast. Rub it with still more salt and pepper.

Brown the butter in a stewing pan on top of the stove. Brown the meat well all round, add some strained marinade and water, cover and let roast on low heat for 2–3 hours or until tender. It is difficult to say for how long, as it depends on the quality of the meat and also on for how long it has been marinated. A skewer should go right through when it is ready. Take it out and keep it warm.

Method for sauce, or gravy: Brown the flour lightly in some fat from the pan, add strained juice and cream gradually, while stirring all the time. Season with a little salt if needed, and serve separately.

DILLKÖTT—LAMB OR MUTTON WITH DILL SAUCE
(SWEDEN)

Use best end of neck in portion pieces—3 lb for 4-5 people. Put in boiling water or stock, bring to the boil and skim. Add sprigs of parsley, some peppercorns, dill and salt, and simmer for just over 1 hour, or until tender. Dish up the meat and keep hot. Strain and skim the stock from fat.

Sauce: Melt 2 tablespoons butter, add 2 tablespoons flour and mix to a golden paste. Remove the saucepan and add hot stock gradually, stirring until the mixture is smooth. Put back over the heat and continue stirring until the sauce is boiling. Reduce heat and let simmer for 10 minutes.

Season with 2 tablespoons distilled white vinegar to 1-2 teaspoons sugar and 2 tablespoons dried dill. Just before serving, whisk a yolk with 2 tablespoons cream, add to the sauce and stir. Pour the sauce over the meat, garnish with fresh dill and slices of lemon. Serve with boiled potatoes.

FÅR I KÅL—MUTTON IN CABBAGE
(NORWAY)

Despite the name, lamb is usually used for this dish. Mutton needs longer cooking time. Either way, it is an economical, popular family dish.

2 lb breast of lamb
1 small cabbage
1 oz flour
8 black peppercorns
salt,
chopped parsley

Cut the meat neatly. Bring to the boil, strain and rinse under cold water. If the cabbage is young, let the meat cook again by itself for $\frac{1}{2}$ hour. Slice the cabbage and put alternate layers of meat and cabbage in a large saucepan (fat pieces at the bottom). Sprinkle flour, salt and a few peppercorns between each layer. Cover with water or the stock from the meat if cooked first, put lid on and let simmer for $1\frac{1}{2}$–2 hours. Some people prefer it re-heated several times. Serve on very hot plates garnished with the freshly chopped parsley.

KÅLDOLMAR—CABBAGE ROLLS
(Sweden)

1 medium-sized cabbage
2–3 tablespoons butter or marg.
1–2 tablespoon syrup
salt, pepper, soy
8 fl. oz stock or consommé

Stuffing:

10 oz mixed mince (beef and pork)
2 oz rice (scant)
10 fl. oz milk
$\frac{1}{2}$ tablespoon butter or marg.
salt, pepper

Rinse the rice, lightly fry in the melted butter, add the milk and let simmer until soft and porridge-like. Season and let cool. Mix with the mince, season again and work until smooth.

Pick off the best leaves of the cabbage and parboil in very little water until flexible, but not cooked. The stuffing should be enough for 10–12 leaves. Put a spoonful on each leaf, fold to a neat package. Put these in a well-greased oven-proof dish, season again, melt butter and syrup together and let coil on top. Brown in a medium hot oven all round, baste with hot stock or consommé and let cook until well done and tender, 1–$1\frac{1}{2}$ hours. Serve from the dish with boiled potatoes.

SPARRISLAMM—LAMB IN ASPARAGUS
(DENMARK)

This is a non-economical party dish to be used in the short season when the lamb is young and asparagus in abundance. In the original recipe, tinned asparagus is recommended.

> *3 lb shoulder of lamb, water and salt*
> *2 oz butter or marg., 2 oz flour*
> *2 lb boiled, cut asparagus*
> *2 egg yolks, 2 tablespoons cream*

Boil the meat in salted water until tender. Slice and arrange on a hot dish, and keep hot, and covered. Skim the fat off the stock. Melt butter in a saucepan and stir in the flour. Add a generous pint of meat stock and asparagus water, a little at a time, while stirring. Let simmer for 10–15 minutes, then thicken with the yolks whisked with the cream. Heat the cut asparagus carefully in this sauce, add a knob of butter and pour over the meat. Serve with new potatoes.

KALOPS—STEWED BEEF
(SWEDEN)

This is the old-fashioned way of stewing, nowadays half-forgotten but nevertheless worth-while trying, in between all the glamorous continental casseroles flavoured with tomato, onions, mushrooms, herbs and garlic. It is a simple family dish, and if my memory is right it used to appear for supper on Wednesdays, many, many years ago.

> *2–3 lb of stewing steak*   *2 onions or 4 shallots, sliced*
> *2 tablespoons flour*   *10–15 whole black peppercorns*
> *2 tablespoons butter, or butter and oil*   *2 bay leaves*
> *salt, pepper*   *About a pint of water, or more*

Cut the meat into thick slices or large cubes. Pound with a hammer or with your fist, according to quality of meat. Roll in flour mixed with salt and freshly ground pepper. Brown in a deep stewing pan on top of the stove with the onions. Add the black pepper and the bayleaves, cover with boiling water; skim if you are fussy. Put a lid on and let simmer a couple of hours or until the meat is tender in a rich, brown, rather thick sauce. A little lager or red wine will make the sauce even more tasty, but neither is necessary. A beef cube or a few drops of soy—also optional.

Serve with either cucumber salad, gherkins, pickled beetroot or lingonberries, and boiled potatoes.

PEPPARROTSKÖTT—BOILED BRISKET OF BEEF WITH HORSERADISH SAUCE

This is again a popular family dish all over Scandinavia. Boil the beef with any available kind of vegetable and herb. Strain, skim, and make from the stock and with cream a white sauce seasoned with grated fresh horseradish. Do not cook after the horseradish is added.

BOILED BEEF WITH SAUCE SACHER

Although Sacher is Viennese the secret of this sauce has leaked out, and is very much used in Scandinavia.

To an ordinary 'roux'—paste of butter and flour—add equal amounts of consommé and cream. Stir to the boil, season with Worcestershire sauce, simmer until smooth, thicken with a yolk and season again with chives.

PERSILJESPÄCKAD KALV—VEAL STUFFED WITH PARSLEY
(DENMARK)

This is an extravagant way of cooking veal, but the result is delicious. It is 'pot-roasted' (term used by Larousse) on top of the stove. The pot should be a thick-based, enamelled iron one. The original recipe is for fillet of veal, i.e. a cut which one seldom finds in England. But leg or shoulder will do—the best quality veal available is usually Dutch. Buy 3-3½ lb. Stuff with the fresh green from a large sprig of parsley, or chervil from your garden. Fry the veal in ½ lb of pure butter! Ten minutes each side, while seasoning generously with salt and freshly ground pepper. Add a tin of non-seasoned Italian tomatoes, and a generous amount of stuffed olives. Mild anchovy-stuffed ones, or the ones with pimento. No water whatsoever is allowed into the pot. When the meat is tender but not overdone it is taken out and kept warm. Let the sauce simmer for yet a while, scraping the bottom of the pot with a wooden spoon for all the flavour from the frying.

Pour the sauce into a hot serving dish, and place neatly carved slices of meat on top. Serve with thinly sliced fried potatoes, or rice.

KALVSTEK I ÖL—VEAL IN ALE
(Sweden)

3½–4 lb leg or shoulder	1 bayleaf
2–3 sliced carrots	2 cloves
2–3 sliced onions	3–4 tablespoons melted butter or marg.
1 half-bottle brown ale	salt, pepper

Place the meat in a deep pot as above. Season. Add the carrots and onions. Pour over lightly browned butter and fry for about ½ an hour until the meat is browned all over. Add the ale, the bayleaf and the cloves. Cover with lid and let simmer for 1 hour or until the meat is tender. Baste frequently. Serve the meat with the strained gravy as it is, or thickened with cream and arrowroot.

SVENSK PANNA—SWEDISH POT

Most dieting sheets to-day warn the customer to keep off fried food. Try this for a change:

Slice veal fillets, pork fillets and calf's kidney well trimmed, not too thinly.

Put in cold water, bring to the boil, rinse in running cold water until the water is perfectly clear. Put back on the stove in fresh cold water with a bouquet garni (parsley, thyme and a bayleaf in a little cotton bag) and a large sliced Spanish onion. Add a chicken cube and salt. When the meat is half done add sliced potatoes and let boil until they are just ready, not mashed. Serve sizzling hot with lots of freshly chopped parsley on top, the bouquet removed.

KALV MED FÄNKÅL—ESCALOPES WITH FENNEL

Lightly brown the escalopes and season. Grease a shallow pan and put in a layer of chopped fennel—one good-sized root should be enough for 4–8 escalopes. Cover with white wine, or stock or consommé. Put a lid on and let simmer until tender—about 20 minutes. Remove the meat on to a hot dish and keep warm. Reduce the juice in the pan, add 2 tablespoons cream and 1 or 2 yolks, stirring. Season carefully. Top with freshly chopped parsley or green fennel and serve with new potatoes and perhaps some asparagus.

KALVFILET OSCAR—ESCALOPES OSCAR

This Oscar was King of Sweden in the beginning of the century, and he was Nr. II of that name. This was his favourite dish—a little expensive, but delicious, and with a certain old-fashioned 'air'.
Cut out or choose 'medallions' of veal and flatten them with your fist. Season well with salt and freshly ground white pepper, dip in flour and shake.
Fry in browned butter or half butter, half oil. Put in a hot silver dish, cover each with Sauce Choron (Béarnaise seasoned with pure Tomato purée). Garnish with lobster and asparagus tips. Serve with fried potatoes.

FINSKA FLÄSKKOTLETTER—FINNISH PORK CHOPS

Brown pork chops in oil/butter or oil/marg. Season with salt and pepper, keep warm under cover. Brown 1 tablespoon flour in the frying fat, add a glass of white wine and a glass of stock or tinned consommé. When thickened add 1 teaspoonful of French tarragon mustard with some diced parsley and gherkin. Put the chops back in this sauce, and serve. Baked potatoes or boiled new ones go well with this dish. Also 'mange-tout' peas.

NORSKA FLÄSKKOTLETTER—NORWEGIAN CHOPS

Lamb chops are the best ones for this dish, but veal and pork can be used with good results. Fry the chops until brown and put them on an oven-proof dish. Whisk the juice in the pan with a little water and pour over the chops. Top each chop with a teaspoon of chopped onion and a slice of Roquefort (Danish Blue) cheese. Don't try mousetrap, the only thinkable substitute is Gorgonzola. Ten minutes in the oven—and the onions and the cheese have mingled into a delicious paste!

BIFF MED LÖK—SWEDISH STEAK WITH ONIONS

For 4 rumpsteaks 3 oz butter or half oil/half butter. 2 sliced onions. Seasoning. Rub the steaks with salt and freshly ground pepper. Fry the onions in half the fat, and keep in a hot dish. Fry the steaks to taste—but preferably underdone or 'bloody'. Serve with boiled or fried potatoes.

Everyone who has visited Stockholm in the summer will remember the white passenger-boats that go out to the countless islands in the archipelago where everyone has a summer-house. This 'biff' is a stand-by in the ships' dining saloons.

KALVSTEK PÅ GRÖNSAKSBÄDD—ROAST VEAL ON VEGETABLE BED (SWEDEN)

4 lb shoulder of veal
½ pint water or light stock
3 tablespoons butter or marg.

salt, pepper, rosemary
4–6 small onions
4–6 young carrots
2 leeks in thick slices
½ celeriac cut to sticks

Grease the baking tin well and arrange the vegetables in it. Sprinkle with salt and pepper. Rub the meat with salt, pepper and rosemary and put it on its bed. Pour over some of the hot water or stock and put the pan in a moderate oven. Roast about 1–1½ hours, basting frequently and adding some liquid when necessary. Do not overcook. Carve the meat when it is ready and put it back with the vegs. and serve from the pan, with potatoes baked in their jackets.

KALVKOTLETT MED SPENAT OCH OST—ESCALOPES WITH SPINACH AND CHEESE
(SWEDEN)

Cover the bottom of a well greased shallow oven-proof dish with parboiled and drained spinach leaves (or the contents of 1 small packet deep-frozen spinach, thawed and drained). Lightly fry 4 flattened escalopes of veal and place them on top of the spinach. Mix in the frying pan 7 fl. oz double cream, 2 teaspoons bread-crumbs and 2 tablespoons grated parmesan—or gruyère cheese. Bring to the boil, pour over the escalopes, sprinkle with more cheese and put under the grill to get golden brown.

KALVRULAD MED BACON—ROLLED ESCALOPES WITH BACON
(FINLAND)

1 lb escalopes, generous
10 oz bacon
½ pint veal—or chicken stock
2 medium sized Spanish onions

2 shallots
2 tablespoons butter or marg.
flour
bouquet garni
salt, pepper

Flatten the escalopes. Cover 3/4 of the surfaces with thin stripes of bacon, season and roll them. Fasten with string or a stick. Turn them in flour. Dice the rest of the bacon, chop the onions and the shallots and fry lightly in a saucepan. Add the rolls and fry them golden all round. Pour over the stock, add the bouquet, put a lid on and let simmer 1 hour to 1½. Remove the string or the sticks and place the meat on a hot dish. Strain the sauce and pour over the meat. Serve with mashed potatoes.

HÖKAREPANNA—GROCER'S STEW
(SWEDEN)

1 large calves kidney
1 lb fillet of pork
2 lb sliced raw potatoes
3 onions, thinly sliced
2–3 tablespoons butter or marg.
½ pint bottle lager
salt
crushed peppercorns

Trim kidney and pork and cut into slices. Grease a roomy oven-proof dish and put alternate layers of potato, pork, kidney and onions in it, beginning and finishing with potato. Sprinkle salt and pepper between layers, dot the rest of the butter on top, pour the lager over the lot and bring to the boil. Skim if necessary. Put the lid on and simmer for at least 1 hour.

To serve: either leave the lid on until the dish is actually on the table, to preserve the flavour. Or add a small glass of brandy just before it is taken off the stove.

STEKT FLÄSK MED LÖKSÅS—BELLY OF PORK WITH ONION SAUCE
(SWEDEN)

Use strips of either fresh or lightly salted pork. Salted pork is more common in the Northern countries. Fry until nicely brown and crisp. Season with salt if fresh. Serve with the following sauce:

Simmer 2 chopped onions gently in 2 tablespoons butter until tender but not brown. Sprinkle with 1-2 tablespoons flour and add milk gradually while stirring, until fairly thin. Cook slowly for 15 minutes, season with salt and pepper. Serve with baked potatoes.

Note 1: During the war when all meat was rationed we learnt to dice the pork, let it simmer in the sauce. The result—'Fläsksås med potatis'—Pork sauce with potatoes was a very popular stand-by.

Note 2: The traditional vegetable to go with fried pork is brown beans. If available in your nearest Delicatessen shop, cook them as follows: Wash beans and soak overnight. Boil slowly in the same water until tender—1-1½ hours. Season to taste with salt, syrup and vinegar.

ÄPPELFLÄSK—PORK WITH APPLE
(SWEDEN)

Sliced belly of pork, fresh or slightly salted—1 1¼ lb
2 Spanish onions
2-3 fine apples

Flatten the pork and cut off rind and fat. Let it melt in the frying pan while preparing other ingredients. Core the apples, but do not peel them. Cut in slices. Peel the onions, slice, and let them slowly get soft in the fat or in butter. Remove the rinds. Dip the pork in breadcrumbs and fry slowly until brown, in the pan. Season with salt (if fresh pork is used) and pepper. Then put pork, onions and raw apple in layers in a shallow casserole or in the frying-pan, use the juice in the pan and add enough water or light stock barely to touch the top layer. Put a lid on and let simmer half an hour. Serve with potatoes boiled in their skins, and let each person peel their own.

AEBLEFLÄESK—PORK WITH APPLE
(DENMARK)

¾ *lb bacon or slightly salted pork*
3 *lb apples*
sugar to taste

Cut the pork or bacon into rashers (not too thin) and fry them crisp. Remove from the pan and keep warm. Core the apples and cut them without peeling into eight pieces each. Put these in the bacon fat in the pan and put a lid on. Simmer until soft. Add sugar and turn them carefully. Serve the pieces of apple and the bacon together, with coarse rye bread.

FLÄSK I FORM—PORK 'PIE'
(SWEDEN)

1 *lb 2 oz slightly salted belly of pork*
2–3 *Spanish onions, sliced*
2 *lb peeled, sliced potatoes (generous)*
12 *fl. oz milk*
rosemary, parsley—chopped
salt, white pepper

Slice the pork and remove the rind. Put potatoes and onions in a well greased oven-proof dish, in layers. Season each layer lightly. Pour over the milk, to barely cover.
Top with the slices of pork, put close together. Sprinkle with powdered rosemary.
Bake in a hot oven about 45 minutes, or until the pork is crisp

and potatoes and onions soft. Sprinkle with freshly chopped parsley.

TEATERSKINKA 1—THEATRE-HAM 1

This and the following dish have got their name simply because they are ideal to serve for supper after theatre. They can be prepared beforehand, and put in the oven while you have a drink.

Soak rather thick slices of ham in sherry, for half an hour or more. Arrange them in an oven-proof dish. Mix thick cream (not beaten) with pure tomato-purée—about 1 tablespoon purée to each 3–4 fl. oz cream. Cover the ham with this sauce, and heat without browning. Serve with peas and/or rice.

TEATERSKINKA 2—THEATRE-HAM 2

Butter an oven-proof dish. Brush thick slices of ham with white wine and arrange them in the dish. Mix thick cream (not beaten) with tomato ketchup—same proportions as above. Optional: lightly fried—or raw—sliced button mushrooms and rings of red peppers. Cover with the sauce and put in a hot oven for about ½ hour or until the cream is *slightly* golden. Serve with a salad of French beans.

KALVFILET PANDORA—ESCALOPES PANDORA

Fry small thin escalopes of veal rubbed with salt and freshly ground white pepper and arrange them in a buttered oven-proof dish. Cut a few slices of ham in strips. Slice raw button mushrooms. Cut green pepper in strips. Spread all this over the veal. Whisk the juice from the frying pan with thick cream and pour into the dish—it should be enough to barely cover. Top with slices of Gruyère cheese, and put in a hot oven or under the grill until the cream is golden and bubbling with the melted cheese. Serve with Mange-touts.

REGATTAKOTLETT—YACHTSMEN'S CHOP
(SWEDEN)

4 pork chops, oil and butter or marg.
8 tomatoes
1 Spanish onion
parsley, dried dill
powdered paprika
thyme
bayleaf
salt, pepper

Rub the chops with paprika, salt and pepper. Brown them in hot frying pan, then move to a saucepan. Fry the chopped onion in the same fat as used for the chops. When it is soft and golden, add the tomatoes, peeled and cut in small pieces. Season with a pinch of thyme and 1 bayleaf. Reduce by boiling for a short while, then add the chops. Season again and let simmer for a few minutes. Garlic fans may add garlic. Those who like Italian food could use rosemary and sage in the sauce. Serve in casserole and sprinkle with chopped parsley and dill. Mashed or boiled potatoes go well with it, but spaghetti is better still.

DANSKA FLÄSKKOTLETTE—DANISH PORK CHOPS

4–5 chops
2–3 tablespoons butter or marg.
3½ oz diced gammon
1 Spanish onion, sliced
1 apple, cut in cubes
7 fl. oz sour cream
powdered curry
salt, pepper

Rub the chops with salt, pepper and curry. Fry quickly in a hot pan in browned butter, add the cream, put a lid on and let simmer

10 minutes. Frizzle apple and onion in butter and garnish the chops with this mixture. Serve straight from the pan, with mashed potatoes flavoured with tomato purée.

PURJOFLÄSK—PORK WITH LEEKS
(SWEDEN)

1 lb 4 ozs pork rashers
1 lb leeks, generous
3–4 fl. oz water
1–2 tablespoons butter or marg.
1–2 teaspoons Chinese soy
sage or rosemary, salt and pepper

Cut the rind off the pork. Rinse the leeks carefully and slice. Fry the pork rashers in a flame-proof casserole. When golden brown, remove them. Fry the leeks lightly in the same fat. Put back the pork, season, add a little water and braise with a lid on, on a low flame 15–20 minutes. Season with soy, and thicken if desired with arrowroot dissolved in water. Serve with potatoes baked in their jackets.

FÅRGRYTA MED LINSER—CASSEROLE OF LAMB WITH LENTILS
6–8 hungry people

3–4 lb middle-neck lamb, 2 onions
oil, butter or marg.
water, beef stock cube
salt, black pepper, bouquet garni
10 fl. oz lentils, approx. (or a packet of 8 oz)
Chinese soy
chopped parsley

This casserole should be prepared in the morning if meant for supper, so that all the fat can be removed before the dish is re-heated and served. The lentils should be soaked overnight. Trim the pieces of lamb and rub with salt and freshly ground black pepper. Slice the onions. Let them 'sweat' at the bottom of a deep cast-iron pot in a little oil. Meanwhile fry the lamb in a frying pan and move from the pan to the pot as each piece is browned. Barely cover with water and bring to the boil. Skim carefully and patiently. When no more scum comes to surface, add the stock cube and the bouquet, $\frac{1}{2}$ tablespoon salt and some black peppercorns. Put a lid on and let simmer for 1 hour, then add the lentils and cook for another hour. Remove the pot from the stove and cool quickly in a cold place or in the sink in cold water, frequently changed. The fat will be set and easily removed after a couple of hours. Heat again 15 minutes before serving and season with 1–2 teaspoons of soy, according to taste. Take out the bouquet and sprinkle with freshly chopped parsley. Serve on hot soup-plates, with baked or boiled potatoes.

FLÄSKGRYTA MED JORDÄRTSKOCKOR—POT OF PORK WITH JERUSALEM ARTICHOKES

1½ lb lean pork rashers or fillet	butter or marg., flour
beef cube stock	1 lb. artichokes
tomatoe-purée, cream	salt, pepper, sherry (optional)

Cut the meat in slices or cubes. Brown in a cast-iron pot and season. Sprinkle with flour and pour over about 6 fl. oz cube stock mixed with 2 tablespoons tomato purée. Add 3 fl. oz cream, single or double. Let simmer with a lid on until the meat is tender. Meanwhile clean, peel and boil the artichokes. Mix them with the meat when they are ready. Season again and add a little sherry if available. Serve with rice.

KÖTTBULLAR—MEATBALLS

There are as many variations of these as there are cooks. Meatballs were even the title of a pop-song some years ago—i.e. 'Mammas köttbullar'.

They can be made small and fairly dry, of family-sized served in gravy and as such a stand-by in every Scandinavian household. During the war we learned to stretch the proportions no end, or rather to a certain point, of using a minimum of meat to a maximum of bread or potatoes. For best results though, this is what I suggest:

> 1 lb fine minced beef (*generous*)
> 1 tablespoon grated onion
> 1 egg
> 3 fl. oz cream
> 1 slice of day-old white bread, 2 in. thick, squeezed in hot water
> salt, freshly ground black and white pepper

Or:

> 1 lb fine mince, 1 egg
> 3–4 dessertspoons toasted breadcrumbs
> 3 mashed, medium-sized boiled potatoes
> 3 fl. oz water, 3 fl. oz cream
> 1 grated onion
> salt, pepper, a suspicion of sugar

Instead of beef only, many prefer ½ lb minced beef, ¼ minced veal and ¼ minced pork.

Optional: a little sherry.

Start soaking the bread and crushing it. Add egg, onion, potatoes if used, and last the meat and seasoning. Beat the mixture well. (Leave to rest for an hour.) Make round balls using wet hands or wet wooden or silver spoons. For frying, use 2–3 tablespoons butter, marg. or oil, or oil mixed with butter or marg. When brown put in the meatballs, fry gently and shake the pan to make sure that they don't stick and get evenly brown. For 'Smörgåsbord' or as a tit-bit on a stick, make them small and drain them from the fat. For a family dish, make them large and use the juice in the pan for gravy, thicken with two teaspoons arrowroot dissolved in water. Finish with a little cream. Serve with 'Lingonberries', a preserve you can find in the big London stores. A good substitute is Cranberry sauce or jelly. Pickled beetroot or gherkins mix equally well with the meatballs.

BIFF À LA LINDSTRÖM—MINCE WITH A DIFFERENCE

For special occasions:

> 2 lb extra fine mince (as for Boeuf Tartare)
> 4 yolks
> 4 tablespoons double cream
> 4 tablespoons diced, cold, boiled potato
> 3 tablespoons diced pickled beetroot (Baby Beets)
> 2 tablespoons grated onion
> 1 tablespoon diced capers
> salt, freshly ground white pepper

For general use:

> 2 lb mince
> 1 egg
> 2 fl. oz cream
> 2 fl. oz water
> 2–3 tablespoons diced, cold, boiled potato
> 2–3 tablespoons diced pickled beetroot
> 2–3 tablespoons diced onion, lightly browned
> 1 tablespoon diced capers (optional)
> salt, pepper

For frying: 2–3 tablespoons butter, marg. or oil, or oil mixed with butter or marg.

Blend all ingredients quickly and season carefully. Make thick round balls the size of an egg and fry in the well browned fat. They should be rosy inside when done. Serve either on toast or with roast potato, or with any mild, fresh vegetable which happens to be the best buy of the day.

Wallenberg is the name of a Swedish family of bankers and sportsmen with a great feeling for culinary subtleties. The most famous Swedish gastronome of the 19th century, Dr Hagdahl, was a relation by marriage. The following seemingly simple recipe is not an invention of his, but carries on the family tradition.

> ¾ lb fillets of veal, cut completely clean from fat, membranes and gristle
> 3-4 yolks
> 7 fl. oz double cream
> salt, pepper
> freshly grated white breadcrumbs
> butter

Mince the veal 3 times finely. Leave to cool in the refrigerator. When really cold, mix in the yolks and the ice cold cream very slowly, stirring continuously. Make egg-shaped balls, flatten them slightly and turn them in the breadcrumbs. Fry slowly and cautiously, arrange on a hot dish and whisk out the juice of the pan with a knob of butter. Pour this over the veal and serve immediately with Petits Pois, creamed potatoes and lingonberries or cranberry sauce.

DEN GODASTE FÄRSEN—THE FINEST FORCEMEAT—MEAT-LOAF

10½ oz fine mince	Top with:
10½ oz minced pork	1 tablespoon French mustard
5 large, non-sweet rusks	1 onion (1¼ tablespoon chopped)
1 yolk	1 tablespoon chopped parsley
½ teaspoon freshly ground black pepper	(1 tablespoon chopped dill)
	1 tablespoon butter or marg.
salt, a pinch of paprika	
tomatoes, fresh, or tinned pimentos	

Soften the rusks in boiling hot water (substitute: 4 tablespoons toasted breadcrumbs). Add seasoning and the yolk, then mix in the meat, stirring steadily. If necessary, add more water. The mixture should be as soft as beaten cream. Grease an oblong mould and put in half the forcemeat. On top of that, spread slices of skinned tomatoes or pimento. If tomatoes are used, season them slightly with salt and pepper. Cover with the rest of the meat and smooth the surface.

Then the finishing touch: Mix all the 'Top' ingredients (the butter must be soft), using a fork. Spread on top of the meat. Bake in a medium hot—or next to hot—oven, for about 1 hour. Watch it and cover if necessary for a little while with foil or grease-proof paper. The surface should not be allowed to get too dark. On the other hand it should be kept crisp.

My English family call this dish 'Mince in gravy'. A very tasty juice comes out of the meat in the mould, and it can be served as it is, direct from the stove, without even dishing up, with new potatoes or mash. The aromatic crust is something quite out of the ordinary. If so desired, put the meat-loaf on a hot shallow dish and garnish with Petits Pois and Spring carrots. Thicken the gravy and serve separately.

GÄSTGIVARE-BIFF—INNKEEPER'S SPECIAL

  1 lb minced pork—generous
  2 eggs
  3 slices white bread
  3 tablespoons chopped onion
  8 oz chantarelles (can be found tinned at delicatessen-shops) or
      mushrooms, diced
  3 tablespoons mild cheddar, diced
  1 tablespoon chopped parsley
  salt, pepper

Soak the bread in a little milk. Lightly fry the mushrooms until their liquid has evaporated. Mix all ingredients well and shape small 'steaks'. Fry them in brown butter.

Poultry and Game

STEKT GÅS—ROAST GOOSE
(SWEDEN AND DENMARK)

1 young goose (10-12 lb)   Stuffing:
½ pint light stock or water   1 lb peeled, cored and sliced apples
1 teaspoon arrowroot   ½ lb stoned prunes
½ lemon, salt, pepper   1 teaspoon ginger (optional)

Remove as much as possible of the inside fat. Wash and dry the
goose thoroughly. Rub with lemon and leave for a short while to
dry. Parboil the prunes. Rub the goose with salt and pepper. Fill

with the fruit (sprinkled with ginger). Sew and truss. Place on a rack, breast up, in baking tin and put in a fairly hot oven (425°F). Pour boiling stock or water in the tin after 10-15 minutes, to prevent the melting fat from getting burnt. Reduce heat after 20-30 minutes. Baste every ten minutes, and add more liquid if necessary. Roast the goose 1½-2 hours if the bird if young, longer for an older bird. It is essential not to overcook. Try it with a skewer—when the juice is a very pale pink or colourless the goose is cooked. When nearly ready, pour over 2 tablespoons cold water or rub quickly with ice cubes to make the skin crisp and shiny. Leave the oven door slightly ajar for the last 15 minutes, and stop the basting. Untruss and remove string and stuffing. Place on a hot platter. Strain the juice from the pan and skim off fat, but do not throw it away. Bring the juice to the boil and thicken with the arrowroot creamed with cold water. This gravy can be seasoned with Chinese soy and blackcurrant jelly, if so wished. To garnish the goose: freshly boiled apples and prunes. Serve with roast or fried potatoes, chestnut purée, and red cabbage (see Roast pork). The fat or dripping from the goose is delicious to spread on bread. Sprinkle with salt.

CHESTNUT PURÉE

1 lb chestnuts	2 tablespoons butter
5 fl. oz light stock	3-4 fl. oz cream
sprig of celery	salt (sugar)

Cut a cross with a sharp knife at the top of each chestnut. Boil them for 10-15 minutes. Shell and remove the inner skin as well. Then boil again in the stock, with the celery, 45 minutes. Rub through a sieve. Put back in saucepan and warm, stirring while adding cream and butter. Season.

GÅSLEVERPASTEJ—GOOSELIVER PÂTÉ

1 gooseliver	suet, ⅛ of the weight of the liver
pork, ⅛ of the weight of the liver	2 tablespoons butter or marg.

1 bayleaf   grated nutmeg
1 clove   salt, pepper

Mince liver, pork and suet and press through a sieve, or colander.
Pound the bayleaf and the clove. Season the mixture and fill a well
greased mould to ¾. Cover with foil or grease-proof paper and bake
in a tin with water, in medium oven, 30-40 minutes.

STEKT AND—ROAST DUCK
(DENMARK)

1 duck (about 4 lb)
½ lb apples
4 oz prunes

Prepare and stuff the duck exactly the same way as the goose, but
without ginger. Cut up liver and heart and mix with the fruit.
Roast the duck like the goose, but for no more than 1 hour.

STEKT VILDAND—ROAST WILD DUCK
(SWEDEN)

1 wild duck   1-2 tablespoons flour
3-4 fl. oz sour cream   3-4 fl. oz double cream
4-5 fl. oz milk   1 tablespoon blackcurrant jelly
1-2 tablespoons butter or marg.   salt, pepper

Rub the bird with salt and pepper. Pot-roast it on top of the stove:
brown it all round in butter with the liver in a small frying pot.
Pour over the sour cream and add the milk—the amount of liquid
should be fairly generous. Cover with a lid and let simmer for 45
minutes to an hour. Remove the duck and keep it warm.
Frizzle butter and flour until light brown, add the strained liquid
from the pot, stir and cook for 10 minutes, gradually adding the
double cream. Season with salt, pepper and blackcurrant jelly.
Serve the sauce separately.

Grouse does not exist in Scandinavia—the nearest thing is called 'Ripa'. But I have found that old grouse is delicious pot-roasted as above, like the wild duck. Alternatively: brown with bacon and let simmer in brown stock. Make the sauce as for duck, with double cream. Or add cream only, after the browning, and let simmer until the grouse is tender. Then remove it and whisk some port with the creamy gravy in the pot, and serve this mixture as sauce.

It might seem quite unnecessary to write about turkey or chicken in a book for cooks of a country where the one is the traditional festive fare and the other tends to be an everyday dish. Turkey is a party dish for Scandinavians too, but it does not belong to the Christmas table. Chickens are as cheap and common—relatively speaking—as over here. But bread sauce is not served with either bird, nor is sage-and-onion stuffing. My first turkey was sent to me during the war from an aunt who lived in the country, and as far as I can remember it was not very large. Still it scared me stiff, thinking that I might ruin such a precious present out of pure ignorance. The few books I then possessed suggested nothing but simple roasting, but I felt that it deserved something more imaginative. The hamper in which it arrived contained real double cream amongst a few other luxuries; bacon was not rationed yet and in my larder I had, like everyone else, lots of preserved wild mushrooms collected in the autumn from the woods. Thus I cooked the following:

SVAMPFYLLD KALKON—TURKEY WITH CREAMED MUSHROOMS

1 batch creamed mushrooms *Smörgåsbord* enriched with the diced heart and liver, lightly fried. Enough streaky bacon to cover the whole top side of the bird, fastened across with toothpicks.

I rubbed the turkey inside and outside with lemon, and then with salt and freshly ground pepper. Then I stuffed it with the cold, thick creamed mushrooms, mixed with the heart and liver. I spread the bottom with butter and covered the top with bacon. Then I placed her in the baking tin and poured a little hot water round her before putting her in the hot oven. After ten minutes I lowered the heat to moderate without opening the oven door. I basted her after half an hour, and again after 1 hour. After 1½ hours I removed the toothpicks and let the bacon slide down into the gravy, to brown the breast properly. After two hours I basted again and left the oven-door ajar for 15 minutes. Then I removed the bird and kept her warm while I sieved the gravy and skimmed off the fat.

She was served with fried potatoes, red current jelly and mixed sprouts and chestnuts.

TURKEY PANDORA

After 11 years in England and adapting myself to the expectations of an English family I stubbornly stick to my relatively short time roasting turkey: never more than 3 hours even if the bird is as large as the oven can take. She is still clad in bacon but now in foil as well for the first two hours, and during that time not basted. The stuffing is a modification of what I find that Clement Freud recommends.

> 1 lb minced pork
> 8 oz chestnut purée
> as much minced giblets as I can lay my hands on (my American friend
>   does not use them, nor does my daily)
> 1 grated onion
> 6 oz white breadcrumbs, soaked in a little water and cream
> 2 eggs
> 1–2 tablespoons brandy
> stock—the forcemeat should only just be stiff enough to shape
>   rissoles
> salt, pepper and chervil

Half the stuffing goes inside the bird, half is fried separately as rissoles.

DUVOR I KOMPOTT—BRAISED PIGEONS

This recipe is from a book published 1879 and written by a very famous doctor and gastronome. I guess that his word 'compote' stands for casserole. The measures he uses are the old ones, and my translation is approximate.

> *4 pigeons, 4 oz pork, cut in cubes, 20 mushrooms, parsley, chives, tarragon, pepper, salt, 15 fl. oz stock*

Use a cast-iron pot and fry the pork lightly, then add the pigeons. When they are browned all round they are followed by the mushrooms, herbs and spices. Then let simmer with the lid on until tender—30 minutes (!). Served garnished with pork and mushrooms and the gravy a little thickened. The doctor finds this the simplest but also the best way with pigeons, and notes that olives can be substituted for the mushrooms, to advantage for the dish. The cooking time needed is naturally longer in England to-day, as the birds available are usually old ones.

OM KYCKLING—ABOUT CHICKENS

In Scandinavia the word 'chicken' used to mean the young bird only—the 'petit poussin'. It was a highly priced spring-time delicacy, which is why many recipes still are headed 'Spring chicken'. The boilers were called 'hens'; every old cookery book has at least one suggestion for the 'Sunday hen'. And the methods sometimes still remain the same, even when our material is to-day's oven-ready, polythene-packed, undistinguished bird.

STEKT VÅRKYCKLING I GRYTA—POT-ROAST SPRING CHICKEN

Use an enamelled cast-iron pot with a lid, just large enough for your number of birds. For 2 petit poussins, mix 2 tablespoons of butter or marg. with 2 tablespoons freshly chopped parsley and the juice from a small grated onion, or 1 chopped shallot. Rub the birds inside and outside with lemon, salt and pepper, then put the mixture inside. Brown them on top of the stove, turning them with wooden spoons, in mixed oil and butter. Then add a generous ½ pint mixed cream and light stock, put the lid on tightly and place the pot in a moderate oven for 40-50 minutes. The old recipes advise basting every 10 minutes, but I don't find that necessary. When ready, cut the chickens in halves, place them in a serving dish and keep warm. Scrape the liver and mix with the gravy, and let boil for some 10 minutes. Then strain the gravy, season and pour over the birds. Serve with fried potatoes and a salad of fresh lettuce.

STEKT VÅRKYCKLING HIRAM—ROAST CHICKEN À LA HIRAM

Again buy petit poussins. Cut them in halves when raw, and remove the thin ribs with a sharp knife. Rub with lemon, salt and pepper. Butter generously a baking-tin or oven-proof shallow dish, which can be taken straight to the table. Heat the oven to at least 450 degs. Heat butter in a saucepan on top of the stove. Place the chickens, cut side down, in the dish, pour over the butter and put the dish in the oven. The chickens don't need basting and should be ready in 45 minutes, or a little more according to size. Towards the end of the time the livers could be added. The chickens should be served well browned and crisp-skinned, piping hot and with no other sauce than the gravy in the dish.

VARIATIONS OF ROAST CHICKEN À LA HIRAM

1. Put a large heap of fresh parsley under each half chicken.
2. Cover the buttered bottom of the dish with a bed of freshly chopped onion, parsley and mushrooms.
3. Add to all that skinned tomatoes, cut in neat cubes.

MEXIKANSK VÅRKYCKLING—MEXICAN SPRING CHICKEN

No doubt this sounds funny in Scandinavian context, but the recipe is included as it is a favourite of Prince Bertil's—himself an expert cook.

Pot-roast 3 poussins. Bone and keep hot. Meanwhile arrange the following bed for them: About 3 fl. oz wild rice carefully rinsed— it is very dirty. Boil in plenty of salted water 30-40 minutes. The same amount of ordinary rice, cooked in its double quantity of salted water 18 minutes. Blend both kinds of rice. Mix with a chopped fried onion, ½ lb sliced fried button mushrooms, chopped fresh green or red pepper, 1 small tin petits pois, strained of its liquid; chopped fresh parsley. Serve hot with the pieces of chicken on top, with the following red wine sauce:

Ideally made of thick stock of veal knuckles, browned and boiled with onions and carrots, strained and reduced. Lacking that, a tin of consommé, thickened with arrowroot and whisked with double cream. Season with wine to taste.

KALL CITRONKYCKLING—COLD LEMON CHICKEN

Boil a medium sized spring chicken in lightly salted water with some peppercorns and a large sprig of parsley. Cool in the stock. Cut in neat pieces and remove as many of the bones as possible. Arrange on a dish and cover with the following sauce:

Whisk 3 yolks with 12 fl. oz cream and 2 tablespoons sherry. Let simmer slowly, stirring, until thick and creamy. Do *not* boil. Season with salt and pepper. Spread the sauce over the chicken and finish off with sprinkling 2 tablespoons of fine strips of lemon rind on top. Put away in a cool place. When serving, garnish round the edge with chopped fresh lettuce—and if possible with fresh chevril. If in a very extravagant mood—decorate with lobster of truffles!

HIRAMS SÖNDAGSHÖNA—SUNDAY CHICKEN À LA HIRAM

For 5-6 people: a larage but lean chicken
½ lb gammon
4 oz white bread

2 eggs
1 clove garlic, or 1 shallot or ½ onion
parsley, salt and pepper
3 leeks
parsnip
1 onion
1 clove
(swede, cube of chicken stock)

Mince the gammon with the giblets and mix with the crumbled bread, the lightly beaten eggs, the crushed garlic or grated shallot or onion, the chopped parsley, freshly ground pepper and a pinch of salt—not forgetting that the gammon might be salty. Fill the chicken with this stuffing, and stitch her up. Put her in a pot, cover with water, bring to the boil. Skim, put in the vegetables and a cube if you want to. Let simmer until she is tender—the time depends on her age.

If she is to be served at once, remove the string and keep her hot while the sauce is made of 2 tablespoons butter, 2 tablespoons flour, strained stock and cream—together a scant pint. Season and finish it off with 2 yolks, after which it is not allowed to boil. When the chicken is served, use a spoon for the stuffing and give each person a fair portion. Rice and a big bowl of fresh lettuce go well with her.

If you want to prepare the chicken on Friday for Sunday—let her cool in the stock. Carve her on the Sunday when still cold, and lift out the stuffing whole. Place in the middle of a greased oven-proof shallow dish, arrange slices and neat pieces on top and around in the shape of a chicken, pour over the sauce, sprinkle with grated cheese and put in a hot oven—i.e. serve 'au gratin'.

OM VILDFÅGEL—ABOUT GAME

Visitors to Sweden are often intrigued by the thick gravy or sauce served with game, and sometimes also with roast chicken. The method can be easy enough—just ample use of cream or double cream, with some unusual seasoning. Regrettably, the strong flavour of the gravy often means that the bird itself has been over-cooked and deprived of its juiciness. One of our famous chefs has a lot to say about this subject. He admits that his method takes some time and trouble, but insists that the result is worth while. He recommends it for *Roast wild duck*, but it is equally good for *pheasant, partridge* and even *grouse*. His main issue is that the bird must *not* be overcooked. When ready, it should be carved as soon as it has cooled enough to handle. Breast and legs should be wrapped in greased paper and kept warm. Then proceed with the sauce.

FÅGELSÅS—GAME GRAVY

Cut the carcase and roast the bones in the pan used for the bird. Fry in a saucepan some chopped onion and carrots and parsley, add a bayleaf, a pinch of thyme and some tomatopuré. Move the bones over to the saucepan and rinse out the bird-pan with light stock (from a cube). Pour over the bones and let boil for 20 minutes, skimming. Strain, bring to the boil again and skim until clear. Now you have a wonderful gravy which can, of course, be used as it is. A few spoonfuls should in any case be kept to pour round the bird when serving.

For thickening use 'beurre manié', i.e. equal amounts of butter and flour, mixed cold. Add a little at a time to the gravy, whisking. Let boil for 10 minutes. Finish the sauce with cream. For seasoning: salt, pepper and blackcurrant jelly to taste. A very particular cook now strains once more, and the most scrupulous even wrings the sauce through a filtering cloth. Serve from a heated sauce-boat.

Vegetables, Potato Dishes, Salads

DANSK POTATIS—DANISH POTATOES

Scrub large potatoes and bake them 45 minutes in moderate-hot oven (400 degrees). When still hot, roll them gently on a cutting-board to make them slightly mashed inside. Cut open and top with creamed butter mixed with chopped prawns or shrimps and dill. Serve as an individual entrée, or with fish baked in foil.

STEKT POTATIS—FRIED POTATOES

Peel and slice and dry large potatoes. Heat butter or marg. mixed with oil in a large frying pan—if you have an ancient cast-iron one, treasure it! Dry the potatoes in a clean cloth and put them into the sizzling hot fat. Watch carefully, shake the pan and turn the slices so they get golden but not burnt, each side. Season after a while with freshly ground pepper and salt, lower the heat and let them cook for about 45 minutes until they are brown and crisp round the edges.

ROAST POTATOES—larger quantity

Peel and dice and dry large potatoes. Brown butter or marg. in the roasting tin, add the potatoes and put in moderate-hot oven. Turn them over from time to time until evenly brown, season with salt and roast until tender, 20–30 minutes. Spray with chopped parsley before serving.

STUVAD POTATIS—CREAMED POTATOES

10 medium sized potatoes
2 tablespoons butter or marg.
¾ pint creamy milk
chopped dill, or/and parsley
or chives or leeks
1 teaspoon salt

Peel the potatoes and cut them in cubes, not too small. Melt butter in a rather wide saucepan, fry the cubes lightly, add the milk and salt. Cover and cook on low heat until tender, 15–20 minutes. Season with the herbs, and serve with gammon, tongue, sausages or smoked fish. Also delicious with pickled salmon or mackerel.
Note: Cold, boiled potatoes can be 'stewed' in thick white sauce and seasoned as above.

RÅRAKOR—POTATO CREPES

10 medium-sized potatoes	*3-4 tablespoons butter or marg.*
1 onion	*freshly ground white pepper*
3 eggs	*1 teaspoon salt*

Peel the potatoes and grate them with the onion. Beat the eggs lightly and add them. Season. Brown the fat in a frying-pan, dab the mixture into it—about a tablespoon each—and fry thin and crisp. Serve with bacon or, as an individual dish, with cranberry sauce! Note: To be still more economical, omit the eggs or use 1 yolk only, and fry in bacon-fat.

RÅSTEKT POTATISKAKA—POTATO CAKE

10 medium-sized potatoes   *4 tablespoons butter or marg.*   *salt*

Peel the potatoes and slice thinly, or grate. Brown half of the fat in a large frying pan. Spread the potatoes neatly, season with salt between layers. Dab remaining fat on top. Cover and keep on low heat for 25-30 minutes. After that time the potatoes should have turned themselves into one solid cake, brown at the bottom. Turn it, using the lid. Garnish with parsley and serve with roast meat, game or poultry, or simply with sausage or bacon. Perhaps a salad? Note: The potatoes can be grated right into the frying pan, with nearly equally good result.

POTATISMOS—MASH, MY WAY

My secret is to boil the peeled potatoes in very little water, seasoned with salt and dill. *Then to keep the water.* Mix the mashed potatoes with butter, cream and that water until light and fluffy, and then season with grated nutmeg—salt and pepper to taste. Optional: a yolk added, with a nut of butter, at the last moment before serving. Note: Left over mash can be shaped into buns, rolled in bread-crumbs and fried. What you get is called 'Potatisbullar' and may be served with spare-rib or sausages.

POTATISLÅDA—POTATO AU GRATIN

Grease an oven-proof dish. Put a thick layer of raw peeled, sliced potatoes at the bottom. Spread with diced onion, grated cheese, flour, salt and pepper. Top with another layer of sliced potatoes. Pour over milk, just to cover. Dab butter on top, cover with a lid or with foil and bake in a medium oven for roughly half an hour. Uncover and go on baking until tender and brown, or for another half hour.

PURJO-POTATIS-LÅDA—POTATOES AND LEEKS

Mix raw slices of potatoes and leeks in a greased dish, season, pour over a little water, cover and cook in a medium oven for about 1 hour.

KROPPKAKOR—'BODY CAKES' OR POTATO DUMPLINGS

10-12 medium-sized cold boiled potatoes	Filling:
1 egg	7 oz chopped gammon
5 oz flour	1 chopped onion
½ teaspoon salt	black pepper

Peel and mince the potatoes. Put them on a board and blend with egg, flour and salt. Fry gammon with onion, season with black pepper and cool. Make a long thick roll of the potato-dough, which should be kept as loose and light as possible. Cut into even, thick slices. Make a hole in each and fill with gammon mixture, then close and shape into round dumplings. Boil plenty of salted water in a wide saucepan, put the dumplings in and boil uncovered until they float—then for another five minutes. Serve hot with melted butter and cranberry sauce, if you can't get lingonberry.

This will serve 4 people—12 dumplings. Left-overs are delicious cut in halves and fried.

Note: A more elaborate version comes from the Baltic Island Öland: Grate 12 raw potatoes. As you work, put them in a sieve on top of a bowl. At the bottom of the bowl you will find some starch, which should be taken care of and mixed with the potatoes after the water has been disposed of. Mix with 5 boiled potatoes, mashed or minced as above. Use only 3½ oz flour and omit the egg. Otherwise proceed as above.

POTATISKAKA MED OST—KÄSERÖSTI—POTATO CAKE WITH CHEESE
(FINLAND)

1½ lb potatoes   5 oz Gruyere cheese (generous)
2 Spanish onions   1 teaspoon salt
2-3 tablespoons butter or marg.

Peel potatoes and onions and grate them roughly. Mix and fry slowly in a frying pan until half done (preferably in two batches). Mix with 2 oz grated cheese and stir until well blended. Flatten the mixture and fry slowly until crisp and brown on bottom side. Turn the cake upside down with the help of a lid and brown on other side. Top with slices of cheese and let them just melt. Serve from pan with lettuce and tomatoes.

HASSELBACKSPOTATIS—HAZEL HILL POTATOES
(SWEDEN)

12-14 oval potatoes
4 tablespoons butter or marg.
2-3 tablespoons dried white bread, sieved (unsweetened, uncoloured breadcrumbs)
4-5 tablespoons grated cheese
2 teaspoons salt

Peel the potatoes, rinse and dry them. Slice them thinly across, *but not quite through*. They should hold together at the bottom. Heat half the butter in a large frying pan, place the potatoes in it, sliced side up, and separate the slices carefully with a knife. Dot with the rest of the butter and sprinkle with bread. Put the pan in a hot oven on a grid and bake, basting every 10 minutes. The potatoes will be soft and brown in 45-50 minutes. Sprinkle the cheese on top just before they are ready. Serve with roast meat.

POTATIS STEKT OVANPÅ SPISEN—ROAST POTATOES ON TOP OF THE STOVE

For this you need a really reliable large frying pan, preferably cast-iron, and looked after with love and care. Which means that it should be cleaned with paper only, or if necessary under running hot water and immediately dried—but never left to soak, and never put into greasy dirty washing-up water.

Peel the potatoes and dry them. Heat half butter, half oil in the pan, put the potatoes in and fry, shaking the pan frequently. Keep the pan hot until the potatoes are brown all round, season with salt and pepper when half done and reduce the heat gradually. The potatoes should be done after 45 minutes to 1 hour—crisp on the outside and soft inside.

POTATISSALLAD 1—POTATO SALAD 1

Dice a couple of large spring onions, using the green as well. Boil them for 1 minute in salted water, drain off the water and then boil them in butter—a lump as large as an egg. The onions should be soft but not take on any colour at all. Season with a tablespoon tarragon vinegar, salt and freshly ground black pepper. Fold in as much sliced boiled potatoes as the sauce can take, and soak through. Serve hot or cold.

POTATISSALLAD 2—POTATO SALAD 2

Good quality potatoes, hard, steamed with their skins on. Peel while they are still warm, cut in rather thick slices, and put in a salad bowl. Damp the slices with water so they don't stick together. Put amongst them a muslin bag with 2 or 3 cloves of garlic. Mix a Sauce Vinaigrette and add to it chopped parsley, chervil, tarragon, chives and capers. Season with a suspicion of cayenne pepper. Pour the sauce over the potatoes and leave for 1 hour before serving. Remove the garlic. The salad is best while still tepid.

OM GRÖNSAKER—ABOUT VEGETABLES

We have no such rule as 'Meat and two vegs.' But we have certain customary combinations—such as onions and carrots with beef, peas with lamb, cabbage with pork, spinach with veal. Celeriac and artichokes (Larousse call them 'winter or Jerusalem artichokes)' are more commonly used than in England, and mange-touts peas very popular when in season. Beans, Brussel sprouts and leeks are used to about the same extent as over here; leeks maybe more in combination with other things: with fish, for instance. Cauliflower is thought to be substantial enough to be served as a dish in its own right, with various garnishings. Mushrooms are enormously popular—all sorts of them are collected wild in the woods in late summer and preserved to last through the winter.

You are not given a choice of for instance potatoes even in the restaurants. Certain kinds 'belong' to certain dishes, as do the other vegetables on the menu.

A big bowl of fresh salad is served with as many family meals as possible. But beetroot is never or hardly ever mixed with lettuce. Chicory is called endives and is as often served cooked as raw. We don't use much watercress but it is increasing. Radishes are served with cheese, rather than celery sticks. Mint is hardly known—but dill is indispensable. Raw tomatoes and cucumber are eaten much more than over here, just as they are.

As the winter is long and hard the really new spring vegetables are tremendously appreciated. The first crop of home-grown potatoes is looked upon as the greatest delicacy. Cooked with dill and served with fresh dill and cold butter it is by many estimated even higher than asparagus.

And I remember many a summer meal with just one big dish with all sorts of vegetables beautifully and colourfully arranged—as follows:

BLANDADE GRÖNSAKER—MIXED GREENS

Centrepiece: a large white cauliflower. Round it small carrots, young beetroots, mange-touts, spinach, spring onions, petits pois. Everything cooked separately in a minimum of salted water for a minimum of time. Garnished with hard-boiled eggs, sliced tomatoes and cucumber, and sprinkled with chopped parsley. Served with melted butter, creamed butter or Sauce Mousseline.

SAUCE MOUSSELINE

2 tablespoons butter
2 yolks
1 tablespoon flour, generous
9 fl. oz veg. stock (not from the beetroots)
juice from ½ lemon
salt, pepper
7 fl. oz whipped double cream

Method as for Mock Hollandaise (see Fish sauces). The cream is added immediately before serving.
This sauce can also at special occasions be served with *Asparagus* or with *Globe Artichoke Bottoms*.

UGNSTEKT BLOMKÅL MED TOMAT—BAKED CAULIFLOWER WITH TOMATOES

1 large cauliflower or 2 smaller   3 tablespoons butter or marg.
water, salt   3 tablespoons grated cheese
3 large tomatoes

Parboil the cauliflower in lightly salted water. Butter a shallow oven-proof dish, put the cauliflower in it with the halved tomatoes around. Dab butter all over, spread the cheese thickly on top and put the dish in a hot oven until beautifully browned. Baste frequently. Serve on its own or with strips of crisp bacon.

BLOMKÅLS-GRATÄNG—CAULIFLOWER AU GRATIN

2 medium sized cauliflowers
water, salt
2 tablespoons butter or marg.

2 tablespoons flour
6 fl. oz cauliflower liquid
8 fl. oz top of the milk
1 yolk
salt, pepper or grated nutmeg

For the top: 2 tablespoons butter, 2 tablespoons toasted bread-crumbs, 3 tablespoons grated cheese.

Boil the cauliflower in lightly salted water, no longer than to the point when it is *just* cooked. Strain off the liquid and keep for the sauce. Place the cauliflower on a buttered dish, whole or divided into neat pieces. Frizzle butter and flour, add the liquid and the heated milk gradually, and boil 10 minutes. Remove from the flame, add the yolk and season to taste. Pour the sauce over the cauliflower, cover the top with breadcrumbs and cheese, dab the butter on top of that and bake in a hot oven just long enough to get golden brown. Serve on its own, or with strips of crisp bacon.

BLOMKÅL MED RÄKSÅS—CAULIFLOWER WITH SHRIMPSAUCE

Shrimps, prawns or crab are in fact equally good with cauliflower. With the addition of any of these to the sauce, the ingredients and the method are the same as for Cauliflower au gratin. One can also leave out the final browning and finish off the sauce with dabs of cold butter instead. If tinned crab is used, the liquid from the tin substitutes some of the vegetable stock.

Selleri—Celeriac is easy to peel, however rough it looks, if cut in slices *before* peeling. It can thereafter be served as any veg. simply boiled, or parboiled and then dipped in egg and breadcrumbs and fried. Any of the recipes for cauliflower mentioned above applies to celeriac. It can also be topped with creamed spinach.

In the old days of large formal dinners, *Celeriac with creamed mushrooms* was a very popular entrée (third course).

Jordärtskockor—Jerusalem artichokes mix equally well with mushrooms, fish and shellfish, as the following recipe for a veg. to be served with any meat.

2 lb artichokes
water, salt
½ pint light stock (cube)
1 tablespoon butter or marg., generous
2 tablespoons flour
3 fl. oz cream, 1 yolk

Scrub the artichokes and put them for a few minutes in boiling water, then peel them. Put them in the boiling stock and let simmer until soft. Strain and keep the stock. Frizzle butter and flour for a few minutes, add the artichokes and so much of the stock as to barely cover. Simmer again for 10 minutes, then season with salt and freshly ground pepper. Finally add the yolk whisked with the cream.

GRÖNSAKSPUDDING—GLORIFIED BUBBLE AND SQUEAK
(FINLAND)

In those days when we are all warned not to eat too much fried food this is a nice way of using left-over vegetables, cooked or uncooked. I found myself the other day with some cooked cabbage, one raw leek, half a swede and about half a pound of 'new' carrots. In this case, obviously anything goes.

I peeled and boiled two potatoes with the cut-up swede, and added the leek and the carrots after a little while. When soft, I roughly mashed it together with a dab of butter and the cooked cabbage. While the roots were cooking I soaked two dessertspoons of white breadcrumbs in 8 oz milk, added one lightly beaten egg and mixed it with the vegs.* Then I put it in a greased oven-proof glass-dish, sprinkled breadcrumbs on top and baked it in a medium hot oven for 45 minutes. Grated cheese will add to the flavour.

When made on carrots only, the Finns call this pudding Porkkanalaatikko, when with swedes Lanttulaatikko.

* Seasoned with salt, freshly ground black pepper and grated nutmeg.

It is important that the lettuce is clean, crisp and dry. After rinsing, shake each leaf and spread them on a big clean cloth. Fold the cloth and press gently. Then put it in the fridge and keep it there until just before blending with other ingredients, and serving.

The most common dressing is of course the classical French: 2-4 measures oil to one vinegar or lemon juice. Salt and freshly ground black pepper. It is also called Sauce Vinaigrette.

AGNETAS SALLAD—SALAD AGNETA

Lettuce, cucumber, tomatoes, red or green pepper, raw mushrooms, radishes, parsley, chives. Everything neatly cut, sliced, chopped. Sauce as for 'Gravlax': 1 tablespoon Swedish or French mustard, 1 tablespoon caster sugar, 2 tablespoons wine vinegar, 3-4 fl. oz oil, salt and pepper to taste. This sauce should be rather thick.

VARDAGSSALLAD—WINTRY EVERYDAY-SALAD

Finely striped white cabbage. Diced winter apples. Grated carrots. French dressing.

SALLAD PÅ SELLERI OCH ÄPPLEN—CELERIAC AND APPLES

Diced, cooked celeriac and diced Coxes. French dressing with ½ teaspoon French mustard and ample seasoning.

SALLAD PÅ RESTER—LEFT-OVER SALAD

Chicken, ham or tongue cut in strips. Cucumber or gherkin, French beans, lettuce, tomatoes, olives (asparagus tips). French dressing.

RÖDBETOR OCH PEPPARROT—BEETROOT AND HORSERADISH

Put alternate layers of sliced beetroot and grated horseradish in a bowl. Mix good wine vinegar with water and barely cover. Leave in a cool place a couple of days. Specially good with stewed beef.

GAMMALDAGS SALLAD—OLD FASHIONED SALAD

Hardboil 2 eggs. It is easiest to shell them while they are warm. Mash the yolks in a bowl with 1 tablespoon French mustard, 1 teaspoon vinegar or lemon juice, 1 tablespoon sugar and a pinch of salt. Stir in 4 fl. oz of sour cream, slowly. A pinch of dry English mustard is optional. Season carefully with freshly ground white pepper. Put lettuce on top of the sauce, and mix the green leaves with slices of egg-whites. Do not stir until the salad is served at the table.

JOPPES RÄKSALLAD—PRAWN SALAD
(REST. RICHE, STOCKHOLM)

This and the following recipe come from the famous Restaurant Riche in Stockholm, where dishes are often named after well-known personalities-about-town.

Mix a generous amount of shelled prawns with raw sliced mushrooms, asparagus tips, cloves of tomatoes and hardboiled eggs, roughly cut lettuce, chopped chives and parsley. Serve with French dressing (Sauce Vinaigrette).

SOMMARSALLAD—SUMMER SALAD
(REST. RICHE, STOCKHOLM)

Big slices of cold fried salmon, cut lettuce, sliced cucumber, cloves of tomatoes, raw, sliced mushrooms, raw cauliflower in bits, sliced radishes, chopped chevril, parsley and chives. All ingredients are mixed well in Sauce Vinaigrette.

VINTERSALLAD—WINTER SALAD

$\frac{1}{4}$–$\frac{1}{2}$ *white cabbage, finely sliced*
2 grated carrots
2 oranges
2–3 tablespoons raisins

Peel the oranges and remove all white and skin and pips. Slice and mix with other ingredients. Season with lemon juice. Serve with various meat dishes.

INLAGD GURKA—CUCUMBER SALAD

This is a special favourite which goes well with lamb, veal and game.

7 oz green cucumber
2 tablespoons distilled white vinegar
2 tablespoons sugar
3–4 fl. oz water
chopped parsley
1 teaspoon salt, freshly ground white pepper

Put the sliced cucumber in a bowl in layers with the parsley in between, finishing with parsley. Mix other ingredients and pour over the cucumber. Leave in a cool place about 1 hour before serving.

SALLAD CARLTON—SALAD CARLTON

$\frac{1}{2}$ *tin pineapple*
1 apple
5 tomatoes
1 stick celery
$\frac{1}{2}$ *cucumber*
lettuce
2 yolks

pineapple juice
1 hardboiled egg
¼ teaspoon French mustard
1 yolk
3 tablespoons wine vinegar
6–7 fl. oz double cream

Whisk the 2 yolks with the pineapple juice in a saucepan (not aluminium). Bring to simmering and thickening, whisking vigorously. Take off the flame and let cool. The cold yolk from the hardboiled egg is rubbed together with the mustard, with the back of a wooden spoon, in a bowl. Add the raw yolk and the vinegar to this, a little at a time. Combine with the cold juice-and-yolk mixture. Finally add the cream, whipped stiff. Season. Cut the fruit and vegetables in neat pieces and slices. Do not mix in the lettuce until the last moment before serving.

ENDIVESALLAD—CHICORY SALAD

Chicory should not be rinsed, as they easily get a bitter flavour from the touch of water. Only remove the outside leaves and cut off the bottom. French dressing of either vinegar or lemon juice. The bowl could be rubbed with a clove of garlic.

TOMATSALLAD—TOMATO SALAD

Slice skinned tomatoes. Place on a plate, sprinkle with salt and leave for ¼ of an hour. Drain. Sprinkle again with pepper, salt, chopped parsley and tarragon. Then blend in a bowl with vinegar and oil. Again the bowl could be rubbed with garlic.

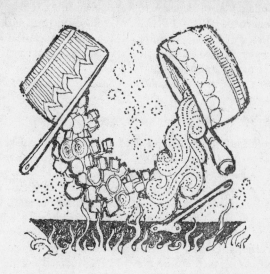

Left-Over Dishes

Most cooks would of course rather have everything they serve
happily finished up than to have to take care of left-overs. Nevertheless, most of us are often faced with the problem of turning
something that looks dry and dreary into something warm and
appetising—which is a special challenge in a country where, by
tradition, lots of people are suspicious of anything 'cooked twice'.
So when you succeed to lure them to enjoy a second presentation
you feel really *good*.

The obvious answers in England when dealing with left-overs of
meat and poultry are either a cottage pie or a curry. I was not
familiar with the former when I first came to live in England, but

will include my method, as my husband seems to enjoy the way it comes out non-greasy. Curry is, of course, international, and again there are as many variations as there are cooks. The one I usually make is called Indian, but is a very mild variation of what it must be like in its home country.

The most famous left-over-dish from Scandinavia is no doubt the

PYTTIPANNA—POTPIECES

The ingredients are equal amounts of diced meat and boiled diced potatoes, some chopped onions and—to enhance the flavour—a little diced bacon. Start by frying the onions golden, put them aside in a hot dish, and then fry the bacon in the same fat. Add it to the onions, clean pan if necessary and then fry the meat. Clean pan again and finally fry the potatoes. Put everything back in pan together and blend carefully. The mixture should not be greasy, but rather crisp. Season, and serve with either beetroot or lingonberry preserve (which can be found in England and is rather like cranberry sauce), gherkin and—optional—fried eggs.

Note: Pyttipanna can also be made of prime raw steak and raw potatoes, and is thereby transformed from a useful week-day luncheon-dish to an excellent and very popular late party supper offering.

(Somewhat to my surprise a very famous English husband-and-wife cooking team suggest diced bread be put in the Pyttipanna. It increases the quantity, but not the quality.)

PYTTIPANNA MARINATED

| 4–5 cold grilled steaks or equal amount of roast beef | 8–10 cold boiled potatoes |
| | 3–4 leeks |

Marinade:

| 2 liquid ounces vinaigre | ½–1 tablespoon 'beefsteak-sauce' |
| 6 liquid ounces oil | (carefully skimmed pan juice) |

Dice meat and potatoes and slice leeks thinly. Whisk ingredients for the marinade together and blend with meat, potatoes and leeks. Chill for an hour and serve. (8 people).

RESTGRYTA—LEFT-OVERS CASSEROLE

Cut boiled or roast meat in small cubes. Fry it with a big onion and a slice of bacon—$\frac{1}{2}$ clove of garlic if you like it. Season with salt, pepper and marjoram and add up to 6 liquid ounces of simple red wine. Boil until the liquid is gone, add a tin of tomato-soup and water to cover. Simmer for a few minutes; serve with rice or mashed potatoes.

RESTGRATÄNG—LEFT-OVERS AU GRATIN

This is a double-covered cottage pie. Cover a well greased oven-proof dish with hot mashed potatoes. Spread diced cooked meat and/or vegetables on top—preferably browned. Sprinkle with hot soup or sauce, season with parboiled diced onion, put another layer of hot mashed potatoes on top, spray with grated cheese and dots of butter. Put in a hot oven 5–10 minutes.

MY COTTAGE PIE

For this I prefer underdone roast beef, minced with an onion. But lamb or chicken will do. Brown slightly in half oil, half butter or margarine. Add stock from the roasting pan, skimmed of all fat. Simmer for a few minutes, put in oven-proof dish.

The Mash: Boil peeled potatoes with salt, mint or dill. Strain and keep the liquid. Mash the potatoes with a wooden fork in their own saucepan, add a knob of butter and stir in single cream and the potato-liquid alternatively until the mash is light and fluffy. Season with salt, pepper and grated nutmeg. Add a yolk of egg, if you feel like it.

Cover the meat with this mash, sprinkle with grated cheese and bread-crumbs and dot butter on top. Put in a hot oven for just enough time to get hot and golden.

Foot-note: This is equally good if not better made with raw mince, and if you have no stock you can use a cube. Serve with gherkins or pickled beet-root.

INDIAN CURRY

Poultry, lamb or veal is used in this curry. For two people, chop and fry one onion until golden, add the diced meat let it fry a few minutes. Add stock and let simmer. Add the following ingredients, modified to taste: 1 dessertspoonful curry-powder dissolved in a little water, 1 dessertspoonful wine vinegar, $\frac{1}{2}$ teaspoon dry mustard, 1 teaspoon worcestersauce, 1 diced apple, 1 tablespoonful of flour, salt, a pinch of sugar and some tomato- or mangoe-chutney. Serve with rice.

MACARONI PUDDING

7 oz macaroni, water
7 oz smoked ham, sausage or left over meat, diced
2 eggs
1 tablespoonful butter or margarine
10 liquid oz of milk
2 tablespoonfuls of grated cheese (Parmesan if possible)
salt, pepper
pepper, grated nutmeg to taste

Put the macaroni in plenty of boiling, salted water and simmer for 20 minutes. Strain and sprinkle with cold water. Fry the meat lightly, add some stock if available, blend with the macaroni, season and put in a greased oven-proof dish.

Mix the eggs and the milk, season and pour on top of the macaroni. Use a fork to make it soak through. Sprinkle the cheese on top, bake in a fairly hot oven for 20 minutes or until set and browned. Serve with melted butter or/and tomato-ketchup.

Foot-note: Spaghetti is better still. And you can mix a little diced bacon with whatever left-over meat.

SILLBULLAR—HERRING BALLS
(SWEDEN)

1 lb soaked, salt herring fillets
2-3 browned diced shallots
1 egg, milk

8 oz cooked meat
2-3 squashed boiled potatoes
pepper

Mince herring, meat, shallots and potatoes. Mix with the lightly beaten egg and some milk to a supple forcemeat. Season with freshly ground pepper. Form egg-shaped balls, roll in beaten egg and breadcrumbs. Fry and serve with potatoes boiled in their skin and the following sauce.

KORINTSÅS—CURRANT SAUCE

2 tablespoons dried currants
9 fl. oz water
2 tablespoons butter or marg
4 fl. oz stock or consommé (generous)
2-3 tablespoons flour
1 tablespoon syrup or brown sugar
2 tablespoons distilled vinegar
salt

Rinse the currants, boil them in the water until soft, drain. Frizzle flour and butter, add stock and let boil 5-10 minutes. Season with syrup or sugar, vinegar and salt. Bring back to the boil and add the currants.

Note: This sweet-sour sauce is just as excellent with salt salmon, salt herring, or tongue.

FORSMAC
(FINLAND)

This is a rough variation of the forcemeat used for 'Sillbullar'. The late Marshal of Finland, Mannerheim, is supposed to have introduced it, possibly from Russia. It is a popular dish to serve in the small hours. Northern parties go on until very late, and it is customary to serve something rather substantial to eat, rather than a drink, for the road. But Beer goes well with it.

Roast 2 lb lamb with a couple of onions. Mince with 6–8 oz raw steak, the onions and 3 fillets of soaked salt herrings and ½ tin of anchovy. (Substitute: 2 fillets of Matjes Herring in brine.) Fry and add some stock, season with anchovy liquid. Serve with baked potatoes.

Desserts

ABOUT DESSERTS

Puddings are rare in Scandinavia, milk puddings most of all, as it seems so much better to drink the milk fresh. Cheese or/and fresh fruit is the common dessert. Still, I remember from my childhood the most wonderful fresh fruit salads, which used to be served after dinner as a refreshment. For some reason it was always the last thing my Mother used to do before changing, even when there was staff hired for special formal parties. And while the supper was in full swing I pinched the banana bits out of the bowl when it was left in the pantry.

Syrup:

½ pint water	3 oranges
4 fl. oz caster sugar	1 grape fruit
juice from 2 lemons	3 bananas
grated lemon rind	3 apples
(white wine, Kirsch)	2–3 pears, 4 oz grapes (generous)
	2 oz shelled walnuts

Boil water and sugar, skim and let cool. Blend with lemon juice and a little grated lemon rind (wine and Kirsch). Peel the fruit and remove all pips, even from the grapes. Toast the nuts. Cut the fruit in fairly large cubes on a plate, so the juice is not wasted. Mix everything in a large glass bowl and serve on ice.

FYLLD MELON—STUFFED MELON

Melon is rather expensive in the Northern countries and more often served as a dessert than as a first course. Try it like this in summer time: Cut a lid off the top of a large cantaloupe. Remove the pips and scoop out the fruit, cut in cubes, mix with fresh raspberries or strawberries and put back. Sugar to taste and a glass of sherry. Serve iced. Garnish with vine-leaves.

ÖSTMANS ÄPPELKAKA——APPLE CAKE AU CHEF DE CUISINE NK

apples
sugar
butter
shelled walnuts, ample

Grease a frying-pan or an oven-proof dish well. Arrange slices of apple in rows, one slice slightly overlapping the next. Sprinkle with sugar. Crush the walnuts—put them in a polythene bag and use the bottom of a bottle. Spread them on top, sprinkle with more sugar and tiny dabs of butter. Bake in slow to medium oven 20–25 minutes, depending of which kind of apple, soft or hard. Serve with cream.

ÄPPELSUFFLÉ—APPLE SOUFFLÉ

    4 apples—sugar to taste—water
    4 yolks
    1 fl. oz sugar
    2 oz scalded, dried, ground almonds (including 3–4 bitter ones)
    grated peel of ½ lemon
    4–5 egg whites

Peel, core and cut the apples in halves. Boil them slowly with sugar and a little water. Drain and put them in a greased oven-proof dish. Stir yolks and sugar together until light and bubbly. Mix with almonds, lemon peel and the beaten whites. Pour over the apple halves and bake in medium oven 20–25 minutes. Serve immediately.

FYLLDA STEKTA ÄPPLEN—STUFFED BAKED APPLES

    8 medium sized apples
    2 fl. oz melted butter
    2½ fl. oz breadcrumbs
    1½ tablespoons sugar

Stuffing:

    30 almonds
    2 fl. oz sugar
    a little water

Grind the almonds, scalded if desired. Pound with the sugar and water until smooth. Peel and core the apples, and fill the centres with the almond paste. Brush the apples with the melted butter, roll them in breadcrumbs mixed with sugar and place in a greased oven-proof dish. Bake in hot oven 20–25 minutes and serve hot with whipped cream.

SVENSK ÄPPELKAKA—SWEDISH APPLE PUDDING

3 large apples
4–5 fl. oz toasted breadcrumbs
2 fl. oz sugar
2½ tablespoons butter or marg.
2 tablespoons water

Peel, core and slice the apples. Butter an oven-proof dish and put in layers of breadcrumbs, apples and sugar, finishing with breadcrumbs. Slice the butter on top and pour the water round the edges. Bake in a medium-slow oven for about 30 minutes. Serve with cream.

ÄPPELKAKA UTAN UGN—APPLE PUDDING WITHOUT THE OVEN
(DENMARK AND SWEDEN)

¾ pint white or brown breadcrumbs
stewed apples (2 lb apples, 8 fl. oz sugar)
3–4 tablespoons butter or marg.
3 fl. oz sugar
jam (raspberry, redcurrant or strawberry)

Stew the apples to a mush. Mix breadcrumbs and sugar and fry golden brown—be careful not to burn. Fill a deep bowl with layers of breadcrumbs, cooled apple mush and jam, beginning and finishing with breadcrumbs. Flatten the surface with a knife, decorate with whipped cream and more jam if desired. Leave to 'set' in a cool place. Serve with cream, if the pudding is left plain.

RINGSTEKTA ÄPPLEN—FRIED APPLE RINGS

4 apples
1–1½ tablespoon butter or marg.
sugar, cinnamon

Core the apples, but do not peel. Slice thinly right across and fry the slices slowly until soft and slightly browned. Serve hot with sugar and ground cinnamon.

AEBLEGRÖD—STEWED APPLES
(DENMARK AND SWEDEN)

3 lb apples
14 fl. oz sugar
water if necessary

Peel and core the apples and cut in small pieces. Boil slowly over low heat and with a lid on until tender. Add the sugar. Serve with cream.

Note: As sauce this can be served with several hot dishes like pork or ham, goose or duck. Piquant flavouring: curry or grated horse radish.

RØDGRØD MED FLØDE—RED FRUIT JELLY WITH CREAM
(DENMARK)

10 servings:

14 oz redcurrants	4 in. vanilla stick
7 oz raspberries	1 glass white wine
7 oz blackcurrants	3½ oz scalded chopped almonds
7 oz cherries	1¾ oz potato or maizena flour
1 lb sugar	per quart of berry juice

Clean and prepare the fruit and mash them with a fork until no whole berries remain. Add 2 pints of water, bring to the boil and let stand for 15 minutes. Sieve. Return to the heat, adding the sugar and the vanilla stick. Bring to the boil again and skim off the froth. Measure the liquid, and dissolve the required amount of potato or maizena flour in the wine and a little cold berry juice. Add the thickening to the boiling berry juice, and remove from heat immediately when it begins to simmer. Be specially careful not to let boil, if potato flour is used. Rinse the serving bowl in cold water, spinkle with castor sugar and pour into it the thickened fruit juice. Sprinkle again with sugar to prevent a skin forming on top. Decorate with the almonds and serve cold with cream.

CRÄDDKAKA—CREAM SOUFFLÉ
(SWEDEN)

4 yolks
3½ tablespoons icing sugar
12 fl. oz double cream
1¾ oz flour
4 egg whites
lemon peel

Stir yolks and sugar together until light and bubbly. Whip the cream and place on top. Sieve the flour on top of the cream and mix very carefully. Finally add the stiff beaten whites. Pour into a large, well greased oven-proof dish, place this dish in a baking pan with water and bake in medium oven about 50 minutes. It is ready to serve when the surface starts cracking. Serve immediately with cold stewed berries, or fruit jelly.

HOVDESSERT—MERINGUE SUISSE—COURT DESSERT

A children's favourite.

8 large meringues
10 fl. oz double cream

Chocolate sauce:

> 6 fl. oz water
> 9 fl. oz sugar
> 6 fl. oz cocoa powder

To make the sauce: Bring water and sugar to the boil. Remove from heat when the whole surface is bubbling and stir in the cocoa. Stir a couple of minutes until smooth. When cold, the sauce will thicken.

Arrange the meringues on a large plate, pour over the beaten cream and, at the last moment, the hot sauce.

VARIATIONS OF COURT DESSERT

1. Dip part of the meringues in melted, cooled-off plain chocolate. Arrange them on a plate in layers, with the beaten cream in between, to a pyramid. Spray with chips of lightly toasted almonds.
2. Flavour the beaten cream with nescafé or very finely ground ordinary coffee. Garnish with pistachio almonds.
3. Cover the meringues with fresh or just thawed and drained, deep-frozen raspberries or strawberries. Dab the cream on top and let the berries show themselves.

PÄRON MED MINT—PEARS WITH MINT

Chill drained, tinned pears. Use the liquid *or* fresh lemon iujce. Heat and pour it over 1 tablespoon dried mint. Leave for an hour, chill and sieve and pour over the halved pears. Two halves and the juice will give you 100–115 calories.

KATRINPLOMMONSUFFLÉ—PRUNES SOUFFLÉ
(SWEDEN)

> 20 prunes
> 10 almonds

> 6 tablespoons sugar
> 6 egg-whites

Soak the prunes in water, and drain when soft. Cut them finely and mix with the scalded and sliced almonds, and the sugar.

Beat the whites stiff, blend carefully with the fruit and pour into a well greased mould. Bake in medium oven about 30 minutes. Serve with vanilla-flavoured, whisked cream.

BRYLÉPUDDING—CARAMEL PUDDING

Just over 1 pint single cream
4 eggs
1 yolk
1 tablespoon sugar
grated peel of ½ lemon or 3 scalded grated bitter almonds

Caramel:

7 fl. oz sugar
3 tablespoons boiling water

Garnish:

scalded almonds ·

Melt the sugar for the caramel in a frying pan, stirring with a wooden spoon until smooth and lightly brown. Pour in the boiling water and stir again until smooth. Line a mould which measures at least 1¾ pint with this mixture.

Boil cream and sugar in the same frying pan as used for the caramel. Add flavouring. Whisk the eggs with the yolk, sieve and add to the cream, whisking vigorously. Pour into the caramel-lined mould. Cover with lid or greased-proof paper and bake in pan with hot water in slow oven (300 F.) about 45 minutes. Let cool in the mould. Turn carefully out on to serving dish and garnish with almonds.

VANILJ-SÅS—VANILLA SAUCE

For every dessert suggested served with cream, Vanilla sauce is an alternative. It is in fact the Scandinavian idea of custard. One can buy vanilla-sugar for seasoning.

2 yolks
1½ tablespoon caster sugar
12 fl. oz milk
1 tablespoon arrowroot (or corn flour)
6 fl. oz double cream
vanilla essence

Whisk yolks and sugar in a basin. Mix the cold milk and the flour in a saucepan and bring to the boil. Pour over the egg-mixture, stirring vigorously. Pour it all back into the saucepan, put over the flame and whisk again until simmering and thickening. Remove and pour back into the basin. Continue stirring until nearly cold. When cold, season with vanilla essence. Finally add the beaten cream just before serving.

Note: If the sauce is taken off the heat before really thick, it will get too thin when cooled.

VARM CHOKLADSÅS—HOT CHOCOLATE SAUCE TO SERVE WITH ICE

8 fl. oz water
9 fl. oz caster sugar
8 fl. oz cocoa

Mix water and sugar in a saucepan and bring to the boil. When the surface bubbles, remove from heat and stir in the cocoa. Whisk for a minute or two until absolutely smooth. When cool, this sauce will thicken.

KOLA-SÅS—FUDGE-SAUCE

9 fl. oz double cream
9 fl. oz caster sugar
6 fl. oz syrup
2 tablespoons butter
1 teaspoon ginger
1 teaspoon cocoa
½ teaspoon salt

This is a large batch of a rich and delicious sauce to serve hot (with ice) or cold with Choux pastry or Meringues. Mix and boil cream, syrup and sugar until light brown and tasting like fudge. Add butter, ginger and cocoa, and bring again to the boil. It should be thick when ready.

FATTIGA RIDDARE—POOR KNIGHTS

For 6 people. This is a children's favourite.

12–20 slices old but not too stale white bread
12 fl. oz milk

Batter:

2 eggs
½–1 teaspoon salt
1 tablespoon caster sugar

For frying:

3 tablespoons butter or marg.
1 teaspoon ground cinnamon
½ pint milk (scant)
4 fl. oz flour

The bread slices should not be too thin. Soak them in the milk and turn from time to time.

Whisk the eggs vigorously with the spices. Add some of the milk, whisk in the flour and the rest of the milk. Take the bread out of the milk, using a perforated ladle, and dip them in the batter. Fry them golden brown. Serve with jam.

PRINTED IN ROMANIA